PRIVATE FOUNDATIONS

PRIVATE FOUNDATIONS

Before and After the Tax Reform Act of 1969

William H. Smith
Carolyn P. Chiechi

American Enterprise Institute for Public Policy Research
Washington, D. C.

WITHDRAWN

William H. Smith is a partner and Carolyn P. Chiechi is an associate in the law firm of Sutherland, Asbill and Brennan in Washington, D. C.

ISBN 0-8447-3127-7

Domestic Affairs Study 23, May 1974

Library of Congress Catalog Card No. L.C. 74-81002

Printed in the United States of America

CONTENTS

INTRODUCTION

The benefits to society from the activities of private philanthropic foundations have often been recognized. Indeed, in its congressionally directed 1965 report on private foundations, the Treasury Department portrayed the role of private philanthropy and the part played by foundations in the following terms:

> Private philanthropy plays a special and vital role in our society. Beyond providing for areas into which government cannot or should not advance (such as religion), private philanthropic organizations can be uniquely qualified to initiate thought and action, experiment with new and untried ventures, dissent from prevailing attitudes, and act quickly and flexibly.
>
> Private foundations have an important part in this work. Available even to those of relatively restricted means, they enable individuals or small groups to establish new charitable endeavors and to express their own bents, concerns, and experience. In doing so, they enrich the pluralism of our social order. Equally important, because their funds are frequently free of commitment to specific operating programs, they can shift the focus of their interest and their financial support from one charitable area to another. They can, hence, constitute a powerful instrument for evolution, growth, and improvement in the shape and direction of charity.[1]

Congress has long recognized the distinctive value of philanthropy by providing tax exemptions for charitable organizations

---

[1] U.S. Congress, Senate, *U.S. Treasury Department Report on Private Foundations, Presented to the Committee on Finance,* 89th Congress, 1st session (1965), p. 5; hereinafter referred to as *Treasury Report.*

and tax deductions for the contributors to such organizations. In 1969, however, Congress decided to scrutinize and re-evaluate charitable giving in general. Its attention was focused in particular upon private foundations which have played an important role during the last several decades in the work of philanthropy in the United States. The result of such scrutiny may be found in the Tax Reform Act of 1969.

The provisions of the act relating to private foundations indicate that the Congress believed that some tax-exempt organizations had abused public trust. To remedy such breaches of trust, Congress enacted a series of legislative controls applicable only to private foundations.[2] Thus, implicit in its decision to control only private foundations is the congressional judgment that those tax-exempt organizations which have a broad base of public support and which are therefore responsive to public opinion did not warrant additional legislative controls.

This study will examine the reasons underlying this congressional determination and the specific provisions adopted by Congress to control private foundations.

In view of the important role of private philanthropy and philanthropic foundations in the United States, no discussion of the provisions of the Tax Reform Act dealing with private foundations would be complete without an analysis of the act's impact on this role. Moreover, since private philanthropy is not an invention of modern American society and since it existed long before governments granted tax privileges to foster charitable giving, it would be appropriate to begin this study by reviewing the history and scope of private philanthropy and private philanthropic foundations.

---

[2] Section 509 of the Internal Revenue Code of 1954, as amended, which will be discussed at length later, adopts a negative approach in defining the term "private foundation" in that it defines what a private foundation is not, rather than stating what it is. Unless otherwise indicated, the terms "foundation" and "private foundation" are used throughout this study in a rather loose sense and refer generally to those organizations that are exempt from federal tax under section 501(c)(3) of the Internal Revenue Code and that receive their support from one individual or a small group, rather than having a broad base of public support.

1
HISTORICAL ORIGINS OF
MODERN PHILANTHROPY

Although the word "philanthropy" was first coined during the Elizabethan period in England,[1] the concept of charity existed in early
cultures. Prior to the advent of the Judeo-Christian commandment
to "love thy neighbor as thyself," men practiced charity toward the
poor and the suffering. Moreover, they used their money in such a
way that their charitable endeavors outlived them.[2]

One of the earliest known and most rudimentary forms of foundation was found in Egypt where the practice of leaving property in
perpetuity to other than paternal heirs was encouraged for religious
purposes.[3] The Greeks and Romans expanded the concept of charity
to include not only merciful giving for the poor and the suffering but
also the enrichment of the lives of those in the community. Organizations or associations for the support of the needy and for other
charitable purposes attained the status of legal permanence under
Roman law around the first century B.C. During the first and second
centuries A.D., the Roman Empire encouraged the existence of these
associations, which were called foundations. With the advent of
Christianity the Church became the principal administrator of charity
which it viewed as a duty.[4] For centuries, the Christian Church re-

---

[1] J. Barlow, *The History of Philanthropy and the Impact of Tax Legislation*
(Princeton, N. J.: Tax Institute of America, 1971).

[2] F. W. Jaqua, "Function of the Foundation in Modern Society," *N.Y.U. Conference on Charitable Foundations*, vol. 2 (New York: Matthew Bender, 1955),
pp. 153, 157.

[3] M. R. Fremont-Smith, *Foundations and Government* (New York: Russell Sage
Foundation, 1965), p. 14.

[4] W. Weaver, *U.S. Philanthropic Foundations: Their History, Structure, Management, and Record* (New York: Harper & Row, 1967), pp. 7-9.

mained almost the only institution in the western world which engaged in private work for the public welfare.[5]

The Anglo-Saxon legal system adopted and further developed the Roman concept of foundations. After the Norman conquest in 1066, there developed in England a system of ecclesiastical courts which achieved exclusive control over the enforcement of men's wills in accordance with the testator's language and intent.

After 1066, a long and bloody conflict ensued between political authorities and the Church, which through these ecclesiastical courts controlled the larger part of all property given for what are now called charitable uses. This struggle of approximately 400 years ultimately broke the power and influence of the ecclesiastical courts and curtailed the charity holdings of the Church.[6] During this period there was a gradual shift from ecclesiastical to secular control that culminated in the Statute of Charitable Uses of 1601.[7] This Elizabethan codification revealed a shift from pious uses to secular works for public good.[8] The preamble of the statute enumerated the objects of charitable giving as follows:

> The relief of aged, impotent and poor people; the maintenance of sick and maimed soldiers and mariners; schools of learning and free schools and scholars of universities; the repair of bridges, ports, havens, causeways, churches, sea banks and highways; the . . . maintenance of houses of correction; marriages of poor maids; supportation, aid and help of young tradesmen, handicraftsmen and persons decayed; the relief or redemption of prisoners or captives; the aid or ease of any poor inhabitants concerning payment of fifteens, setting out of soldiers and other taxes.

The creation of charitable trusts flourished during the seventeenth century following the passage of the Statute of Charitable Uses. At the same time, the age of American colonization arrived and the settlers of the New World brought philanthropy with them as part of their heritage. The problems and challenges facing the American colonists were instrumental in shaping the goals of American giving and, in time, philanthropy in America "took such firm root and grew

---

[5] Jaqua, "Function of the Foundation," p. 156.

[6] Fremont-Smith, *Foundations and Government*, pp. 16-17.

[7] 43 Eliz. I, c. 4 (1601).

[8] H. A. Moe, "Notes on the Origin of Philanthropy in Christendom," *Proceedings of the American Philosophical Society* (Philadelphia: American Philosophical Society, 1961), p. 146.

4

so prodigiously that it easily assumed a stature and significance all its own."[9]

Although the practice of philanthropy in America has varied with the problems of successive historical epochs, Americans have consistently demonstrated a willingness to give generously for social improvements. Freedom and individual activity have always been characteristic of the American way of life. One of the most famous advocates of individualism, Benjamin Franklin, actively sought to improve social conditions through voluntary associations. For example, he helped to organize a number of civic projects through the Junto, a club for the mutual improvement of its members. He also organized a volunteer fire company, devised methods to pave, clean, and light the streets of Philadelphia, sponsored a plan for policing the city, and played a major role in establishing the academy which later became the University of Pennsylvania.

> Franklin demonstrated that the sovereign remedy of self-help could be applied with equally beneficial results to society. He did not invent the principle of improving social conditions through voluntary associations, but more than any other American before him he showed the availability, usefulness, and appropriateness of that method to American conditions. The voluntary method, as Franklin's success with it suggested . . . was precisely suited to the inclinations of his countrymen.[10]

After a visit to the United States in 1831, Alexis de Tocqueville was astonished by the ample willingness of Americans to support various social improvements so generously. He observed that it was the individual or several individuals in voluntary association who attempted to improve society. His observations led him to conclude that there is some inherent relationship between democratic equality and the voluntary association of citizens for the public welfare and that the health of a democratic nation could be measured by the quality of the functions which its citizens perform.[11]

The nineteenth century witnessed the increased use of private corporations rather than trusts to hold funds for charitable purposes. In 1847 Congress incorporated what has been referred to as the first American corporate foundation—the Smithsonian Institution.[12]

---

[9] R. H. Bremmer, *American Philanthropy* (Chicago: University of Chicago Press, 1966), p. 7.

[10] Ibid., pp. 18-19.

[11] A. C. Marts, *The Generosity of Americans* (Englewood Cliffs, N. J.: Prentice-Hall, 1966), pp. 10, 178.

[12] Jaqua, "Function of the Foundation," p. 159.

This was the first time that Congress had been asked to decide a question regarding American philanthropy, and it has been viewed as a turning point in the history of American philanthropy.[13]

In 1889, an article entitled "Wealth," authored by Andrew Carnegie, was published in *North American Review*. This essay, which was addressed to the leaders of American business and industry, proposed that the rich administer their wealth as a public trust during life rather than bequeathing it to their heirs. It reminded the rich of their responsibilities to society and encouraged them to implement these responsibilities.[14]

It was after the publication of this essay that foundations as we know them today first emerged. Aside from the sense of public trusteeship which Andrew Carnegie advocated, one of the contributing factors to the burgeoning of the foundation movement in America was a surplus of wealth among some Americans around the end of the nineteenth century. Moreover, the corporation emerged as a legal form particularly suited to preserving wealth and devoting it to the charitable purposes selected by the donor.[15]

In contrast to the charitable trusts which had earlier been established for narrowly defined purposes, the major foundations created during the first few decades of the twentieth century were established for broad purposes such as the advancement of knowledge and human welfare. These foundations advocated a basic attack on the causes of human misery rather than on the alleviation of its undesirable results, and this new emphasis led to research as a primary activity of foundations.[16]

Voluntary philanthropy in the United States has been claimed to be the essence of our free enterprise system.[17] Foundations, which have increased in number throughout this century and in particular during the last thirty years, have assumed a vital role because it was recognized that philanthropy could be most efficiently carried out in an organized form.[18] The advantages of organization therefore make foundations a more effective tool in the voluntary philanthropic

---

[13] J. Lankford, *Congress and the Foundation in the Twentieth Century* (River Falls: Wisconsin State University, 1964), pp. 4-6.

[14] Bremmer, *American Philanthropy*, p. 106.

[15] Jaqua, "Function of the Foundation," p. 160.

[16] Weaver, *U.S. Philanthropic Foundations*, p. 25.

[17] E. C. Jenkins, *Philanthropy in America* (New York: Association Press, 1950), p. 5.

[18] *The Foundation Directory*, 4th ed. (New York: Columbia University Press, 1971), indicates that there were approximately 26,000 active American foundations in 1971.

system than individuals. Among these advantages are "continuity, certainty of the availability of funds, the possibility of professional staffing, and the bringing to bear upon selected problems of larger sums of money—and therefore a broader and stronger array of talents—than individual efforts . . . [are] able to supply."[19]

Private foundations are one component of what has been referred to as the "independent sector"—the thousands of interrelated institutions and organizations which are distinguished from business and industry on the one hand and from government on the other.[20] It is precisely this independence or freedom possessed by foundations which makes them of distinctive value to American society, for it enables them to undertake the new and innovative programs that cannot usually attract a wide base of philanthropic support.[21]

The Treasury report of 1965 summarized the unique role of private philanthropic foundations in American society as follows:

> Private philanthropic organizations can possess important characteristics which modern government necessarily lacks. They may be many-centered, free of administrative superstructure, subject to the readily exercised control of individuals with widely diversified views and interests. Such characteristics give these organizations great opportunity to initiate thought and action, to experiment with new and untried ventures, to dissent from prevailing attitudes, and to act quickly and flexibly. Precisely because they can be initiated and controlled by a single person or a small group, they may evoke great intensity of interest and dedication of energy. These values, in themselves, justify the tax exemptions and deductions which the law provides for philanthropic activity.
>
> Private foundations play a significant part in the work of philanthropy. While the foundation is a relatively modern development, its predecessor, the trust, has ancient vintage. Like its antecedent, the foundation permits a donor to commit to special uses the funds which he gives to charity.

---

[19] Statement of Messrs. J. G. Harrar, A. Pifer, and D. Freeman, in U.S. Congress, Senate, *Hearings on H.R. 13270 before the Committee on Finance to Reform the Income Tax Laws*, 91st Congress, 1st session (1969), pt. 6, pp. 5465, 5467; hereinafter cited as *Senate Hearings*.

[20] M. M. Pattillo, Jr., "Implications of the Act," in *Tax Problems of Non-Profit Organizations*, ed. G. Webster and W. Lehrfeld (New York: The Journal of Taxation, 1970), pp. 191-193.

[21] D. Creel, "Problems Posed for Larger Foundations," in *Tax Problems of Non-Profit Organizations*, pp. 181-186.

Rather than being compelled to choose among the existing operating organizations, he can create a new fund, with its own areas of interest and emphasis. His foundation may encourage existing operating organizations to develop in new directions, or it may lead to the formation of new organizations. Even if it does neither, it reflects the bents, the concerns, and the experience of its creator; and it thereby increases the diversity of charitable works. In these ways, foundations have enriched and strengthened the pluralism of our social order.

Private foundations have also preserved fluidity and provided impetus for change within the structure of American philanthropy. Operating charitable organizations tend to establish and work within defined patterns. The areas of their concern become fixed, their goals set, their major efforts directed to the improvement of efficiency and effectiveness within an accepted framework. Their funds are typically consigned to definite—and growing—budgets. The assets of private foundations, on the other hand, are frequently free of commitment to specific operating programs or projects; and that freedom permits foundations relative ease in the shift of their focus of interest and their financial support from one charitable area to another. New ventures can be assisted, new areas explored, new concepts developed, new causes advanced. Because of its unique flexibility, then, the private foundation can constitute a powerful instrument for evolution, growth, and improvement in the shape and direction of charity.[22]

The contribution that philanthropic foundations make to the common welfare has been recognized through the public policy of exempting them from the income tax. "The American people have wanted to encourage public-spirited voluntary giving in order to assure a variety of sources of support for activities that are for the common welfare. We have not wanted such activities to be wholly dependent on tax funds. This is the reason for the tax exemption of foundations." [23]

---

[22] *Treasury Report*, pp. 12-13.

[23] Statement of M. M. Pattillo, Jr., in U.S. Congress, House of Representatives, *Hearings before the Committee on Ways and Means on the Subject of Tax Reform*, 91st Congress, 1st session (1969), pt. 1, pp. 83, 84; hereinafter cited as *House Hearings*.

2

FEDERAL INCOME TAX
EXEMPTION OF CHARITABLE
ORGANIZATIONS

Although the first statute exempting charitable organizations from federal income tax was not enacted until 1894, such organizations had been exempted from property taxes much earlier.[1] The colonial governments decided to exempt churches from property taxes—a practice continued by the states following the American Revolution. As a corollary to the exemption of churches from property taxes, both the colonies and the states fostered the growth of educational institutions by granting them exemption from property taxes. By 1890, "the principle of exemption of educational institutions from taxation . . . was so grounded in the nature of our Government as to represent a practically irrevocable law."[2]

During the nineteenth century, as organizations or institutions began to assume a more important role in carrying out charitable work for the relief of the poor, sick, and needy, the states soon recognized the value of this work and granted tax exemption to such charitable institutions. State and municipal governments came to regard private relief as more effective and efficient than their own efforts.

> But insofar as the State permitted private institutions to take over the work of charity, the latter was *pro tanto* relieving the State of a burden which it had avowedly undertaken to bear. Private institutions were thus performing a public

---

[1] Many of the facts regarding the historical background of the federal income tax exemption have been obtained from C. Belknap and P. Mandel, *The Federal Income Tax Exemption of Charitable Organizations: Its History and Underlying Policy* (New York: The Rockefeller Foundation, 1954).

[2] Blackmar, *History of Federal and State Aid to Higher Education in the United States* (1890), p. 25, quoted in Belknap and Mandel, *Federal Income Tax Exemption of Charitable Organizations*, p. 10.

function. This *quid pro quo* which the private institutions received was immunity from taxation. But it must be observed that what is done here is to state the terms of a bargain which we have not before us. It is not to be supposed that the bargain was openly made and publicly declared. There is no direct evidence that such a bargain was ever made. The process of exempting these private institutions developed imperceptibly, subtly. It was a spontaneous process, leaving no trace of its origin or immediate development.[3]

The practice and underlying policy of granting tax exemption to charitable organizations was therefore firmly entrenched in the United States by 1894, the year that Congress enacted the first income tax statute. Moreover, the fact that England had used the income tax for approximately 100 years and had granted exemption to organizations having charitable purposes presumably also influenced congressional thought in 1894.[4] Section 32 of the Act of 1894 provided in part as follows: "there shall be . . . levied . . . a tax of two per centum annually on the net profits or income above actual operating and business expenses . . . of all . . . corporations, companies, or associations doing business for profit. . . ."[5]

Exemptions from the foregoing provision were granted to charitable, religious, and educational organizations in the following terms:

nothing herein shall apply to . . . corporations, companies, or associations organized and conducted solely for charitable, religious, or educational purposes . . . nor to the stocks, shares, funds, or securities held by any fiduciary or trustee for charitable, and religious, or educational purposes. . . .[6]

Although the Supreme Court declared the Act of 1894 unconstitutional in *Pollock* v. *Farmers' Loan & Trust Co.*, 158 U.S. 601

---

[3] Adler, *Historical Origin of Tax Exemption of Charitable Institutions* (1922), p. 73, quoted in Belknap and Mandel, *Federal Income Tax Exemption of Charitable Organizations*, p. 11.

[4] Belknap and Mandel, *Federal Income Tax Exemption of Charitable Organizations*, p. 13. The English courts interpreted the word "charitable" very broadly. The first comprehensive judicial definition of charity is that of Lord Macnaghten in Commissioners of Income Tax v. Pemsel, A.C. 531, 583 (1891): "Charity in its legal sense comprises four principal divisions: trusts for the relief of poverty; trusts for the advancement of education; trusts for the advancement of religion; and trusts for other purposes beneficial to the community, not falling under any of the preceding heads."

[5] Act of August 15, 1894, 28 Stat. 553, c. 349.

[6] Ibid., section 32.

(1895), subsequent tax legislation has contained exemptions based on the wording of the Act of 1894.

The Corporate Excise Tax Act of 1909 imposed a tax on the privilege of doing business.[7] Despite the argument made by some senators at that time that no specific provision was necessary to protect nonprofit charitable organizations from a tax imposed on corporations for profit,[8] Senator Bacon of Georgia, the primary advocate of the exemption provisions, insisted on inserting the exemption language in the 1909 act because of his doubts as to whether charitable organizations were by definition beyond the scope of a corporate profits tax.[9]

Senator Bacon's perseverance was rewarded. As finally enacted, the Corporate Excise Tax of 1909 provided that:

> Every corporation, joint stock company or association, organized for profit and having capital stock, represented by shares, and every insurance company . . . shall be subject to pay annually a special excise tax with respect to the carrying on or doing business . . . *provided,* however, that nothing in this section contained shall apply to . . . any corporation or association organized and operated exclusively for religious, charitable, or educational purposes, no part of the net income of which inures to the benefit of any private stockholder or individual.

The Sixteenth Amendment to the Constitution [10] set the stage for the enactment of the Revenue Act of 1913 which imposed an income tax on individuals, corporations, joint stock companies, associations, and insurance companies. The language of the exemp-

---

[7] 36 Stat. 11, c. 6 (1909).

[8] *The Congressional Record,* vol. 44 (1909), pp. 4148-4149.

[9] During the debates on the 1909 act, Senator Bacon, in response to the question whether or not charitable organizations are exempted by the words "corporation, joint stock company, or association organized for profit," stated: "I think not, Mr. President. I gave the illustration of the Methodist Book Concern for that reason. It is organized for profit, but it is not organized for individual profit. It is organized to make a profit to extend religious work and to extend benevolent work, charitable work, and educational work. It is organized for profit, and does make a profit. That is the very reason why I think the words of the amendment with reference to a corporation tax are not sufficient." Ibid., p. 4151.

[10] The Sixteenth Amendment, which was ratified in February 1913, provides: "The Congress shall have power to lay and collect taxes on incomes, from whatever source derived, without apportionment among the several States, and without regard to any census or enumeration."

tion contained in the Corporate Excise Tax Act of 1909, with the addition of the word "scientific," was repeated in the 1913 act.[11]

Curiously, trusts were not accorded exempt status until the Revenue Act of 1921 added the words "community chest, fund, or foundation" to the exemption provision.[12] This absence was apparently an oversight on the part of Congress and was attributable in all likelihood to the exemption provision having had its genesis in the Corporate Excise Tax Act of 1909.[13]

The terms "literary," [14] "prevention of cruelty to children or animals," [15] and "testing for public safety" [16] were eventually added to the descriptive phrase in the income tax exemption provision. In 1934, a qualification with respect to political activity first appeared as part of the provision,[17] although such activity up to that time had been regarded by administrative and judicial decisions as grounds for denial of exemption.[18]

To support its effort to encourage contributions to charitable organizations, Congress in 1917 added a provision permitting individuals to deduct from income the contributions made to exempt charitable organizations.[19] An estate tax deduction was also enacted in the following year,[20] and a gift tax deduction soon followed.[21] It was in 1935 that corporations were first permitted to take an income tax deduction for charitable contributions.

The foregoing exemption and deduction provisions are today found in sections 501(c)(3), 170(c), 642(c), 2055, 2522 of the Internal Revenue Code of 1954. These provisions assist charitable organizations by relieving them from paying taxes and by encouraging

---

[11] 38 Stat. 114 (1913). The exemption language was: "Provided, however, that nothing in this section shall apply to . . . any corporation or association organized and operated exclusively for religious, charitable, scientific, or educational purposes, no part of the net income of which inures to the benefit of any private stockholder or individual. . . ." 38 Stat. 166, section II G(a).

[12] 42 Stat. 227 (1921).

[13] K. C. Eliasberg, "Charity and Commerce: Section 501(c)(3)—How Much Unrelated Business Activity?" Tax Law Review, vol. 21, no. 21 (1965), pp. 53, 57.

[14] 42 Stat. 227, section 231 (1921).

[15] 40 Stat. 1057, section 231 (1918).

[16] Act of August 16, 1954, 68 A Stat., c. 736, generally known as the Internal Revenue Code of 1954.

[17] Act of 1934, 48 Stat. 680.

[18] Fremont-Smith, Foundations and Government, p. 65.

[19] 40 Stat. 300, section 1201(2) (1917).

[20] Public Law 254, title IV, section 403(a)(3) (1918).

[21] Public Law 176, title III, part II, section 321(a)(2) (1924).

generous donations from potential contributors. Taken together, they indicate a legislative policy of assistance and encouragement to charitable organizations, a policy adhered to since the first exemption provision appeared in the Act of 1894.[22]

---

[22] Belknap and Mandel, *Federal Income Tax Exemption of Charitable Organizations.*

3
CONGRESSIONAL INTEREST
IN FOUNDATIONS

It is interesting to note that the charitable exemption and deduction provisions were originally accepted and, for some time, continued with very little congressional debate. Indeed, prior to 1940 there existed very little congressional interest in charitable organizations and their activities, except for a brief period from 1910 to 1916, when considerable public attention was focused on foundations. The initial cause of this attention was the attempt by members of the Rockefeller family to secure a federal charter of incorporation for the Rockefeller Foundation. After three years of effort with little success, the Rockefellers turned to local government and on April 24, 1913, obtained a charter from the state of New York.[1]

The hostility and distrust of Congress and the public toward organized philanthropy, and in particular toward the Rockefeller Foundation, must be viewed against the background which existed at that time—a background of increasing distrust of big business and the accumulation of wealth. In a period of trust-busting and fear of monopolies, foundations were condemned as instruments of wealth and big business. It was in this climate that Congress empowered the President in April 1912 to create the Commission on Industrial Relations which was given the mandate to inquire into the general condition of labor in the principal industries of the United States.

The commission, whose chairman was Frank P. Walsh, was composed of representatives of labor, management, and the general public. From 1913 to 1915 it conducted hearings on a broad range of subjects, including the concentration of wealth and influence. In 1916 the Walsh Commission, as it was known, published its final

---

[1] Lankford, *Congress and the Foundation*, pp. 8-19.

report in which it accused large foundations of being nothing more than the instruments of wealthy industrialists who desired to control the social and educational aspects of American life through the universities. A majority of the commission recommended censure of many aspects of foundations and proposed, among other things, limitations on the size, income, and life of foundations.[2]

Congress took no steps to implement the Walsh Commission's recommendations, but rather adopted a laissez faire attitude toward foundations until the early 1940s when their number and size began to multiply, causing a revival of congressional and public interest in them. The depression, World War II, and tax advantages no doubt contributed to this relatively sudden expansion of the activities of foundations.

With the increase in the number of foundations came an increase in the abuse of tax privileges. Congress became concerned over the income-producing aspects of various foundation activities that were unrelated to the charitable purposes for which foundations were created. It was during this period of renewed interest in foundations that Congress came to understand that it knew very little about them. For the first time, in 1943, it decided to require information returns to be filed by certain tax-exempt organizations.[3] All foundations were subject to this filing requirement except certain tax-exempt organizations, that is, religious organizations, organizations operated, supervised, or controlled by or in connection with religious organizations, educational organizations,[4] and organizations primarily supported by contributions from the public.

The purpose of Congress in requiring returns from foundations was to enable a thorough study to be made with a view toward legislation. By 1950, armed with the knowledge that some tax-exempt foundations had been used for private profit, Congress was ready to legislate. That knowledge, coupled with the judicial conflict over whether an organization which engaged in unrelated business activities was organized and operated exclusively for exempt charitable purposes, set the stage for the Revenue Act of 1950.[5]

---

[2] Ibid., pp. 20-32 and *Industrial Relations: Final Report and Testimony Submitted to Congress by Senate Committee on Industrial Relations*, 64th Congress, 1st session (1916).

[3] House Report No. 871 to accompany H.R. 3687, 78th Congress, 1st session (1943), pp. 24-25.

[4] An educational organization is one with a regular faculty and curriculum, student body, and campus.

[5] 64 Stat. 947 (1950).

The congressional reaction to the abuses which existed at that time was to enact a series of restrictions on the activities of foundations and certain other tax-exempt organizations, rather than to modify in any way the basic framework of the exemption provisions. These restrictions were re-enacted as sections 502, 503, 504, and 511 to 514 of the Internal Revenue Code of 1954, prior to its amendment by the Tax Reform Act of 1969.[6]

Two of the restrictions imposed by the Revenue Act of 1950 provided for loss of tax-exempt status if the tax-exempt organization engaged in certain prohibited transactions or if it accumulated an unreasonable amount of income. These two restrictions, which were embodied in sections 503 and 504, respectively, were made applicable only to certain types of tax-exempt charitable organizations. Generally, all section 501(c)(3) organizations were made subject to the restrictions. However, the exceptions, which considerably narrowed the scope of applicability of these provisions, provided that the prohibited transactions and unreasonable accumulation rules were not to be applied to the following: (1) religious organizations, other than in the form of a trust, (2) educational organizations maintaining a regular faculty and curriculum and having an enrolled student body, (3) organizations that receive a substantial part of their support from the general public, (4) organizations operated or supported by a religious body if that body is not subject to the "prohibited transactions" or "unreasonable accumulation" rules and (5) a hospital or medical care organization or one engaged in medical education or medical or agricultural research.

As reflected by these categories of exceptions to the rules of sections 503 and 504, those section 501(c)(3) organizations that were publicly supported, in contradistinction to privately supported ones, were expressly not subject to the new rules. Congress believed that by virtue of their public nature such public organizations were not likely to become involved in any of the transactions proscribed by sections 503 and 504.[7]

Before examining how these two provisions in the Revenue Act of 1950 affect foundations, it is worthwhile, as will become evident from the later discussion of the foundation provisions of the Tax Reform Act of 1969, to consider the abuses existing in 1950 and the

---

[6] All statutory references in connection with the Revenue Act of 1950 will be to the provisions of that act as they were re-enacted by the Internal Revenue Code of 1954, before amendment by the Tax Reform Act of 1969.

[7] Senate Report No. 2375, 81st Congress, 2d session (1950), p. 37.

proposals to cure them which were drafted by the House Committee on Ways and Means but did not become law.

One of the abuses of particular interest to Congress in 1950 relates to the donors and trustees of exempt foundations and trusts who derived substantial benefits from their dealings with these organizations. The benefits took a variety of forms, including payment of excessive salaries, loans of funds with abnormally low interest rates, and the purchase and sale of stock or other property at prices beneficial to the donors and trustees but detrimental to the trusts or foundations. In order to check these abuses, the Ways and Means Committee's draft of the Revenue Act of 1950 prohibited, at the risk of loss of exemption, all loans, substantial purchases, and substantial sales of property between a foundation and a substantial contributor or any officer, director, trustee, or their families.[8] The Ways and Means Committee further recommended denying charitable deductions to donors unless the instrument under which the recipient tax-exempt organization was established affirmatively provided that (1) no part of the organization's assets could be loaned to its substantial donors or to any of its officers or trustees or any member of their families or to a corporation controlled by them; (2) only a reasonable compensation for services actually rendered could be paid to such persons by the organization; (3) the services of the organization could not be made available to such persons on a preferential basis; (4) no substantial part of the organization's assets could be used to purchase securities or other property from such persons; and (5) no substantial part of the property could be sold to such persons.[9]

While the Senate Committee on Finance expressed its sympathy with the goals sought by the provisions of the House Committee on Ways and Means, it also believed that such provisions would have been unduly harsh in their application. The Finance Committee did not object to a tax-exempt foundation's engaging in the types of transactions prohibited by the House, as long as the transactions were carried out at arm's length. Furthermore, it recognized the difficulty or impossibility of amending instruments to prohibit engaging in specified transactions.[10]

The Committee on Finance approved, and the Senate adopted, a provision which would prohibit only certain transactions between a foundation and its donor and certain related parties. Transactions

---

[8] See House Report No. 2319, 81st Congress, 2d session (1950), p. 42.
[9] Ibid.
[10] Senate Report No. 2375, p. 37.

between a foundation and its officers, directors, or trustees were not proscribed. The Senate version was adopted and became part of the Revenue Act of 1950. This provision, which was re-enacted as section 503 of the 1954 code, established an arm's-length standard applicable to certain classes of transactions.[11] Violation of section 503 would have resulted in loss of tax-exempt status for a minimum of one taxable year. Interestingly, section 503 did not "absolutely prohibit any specific classes of transactions. Rather, it merely [imposed] statutory arm's-length standards on certain types of transactions."[12]

The "prohibited transactions" were defined in section 503(c) as those in which a foundation in relation to a donor and certain related persons

(1) lends any part of its income or corpus without the receipt of adequate security and a reasonable rate of interest;

(2) pays any compensation in excess of a reasonable allowance for salaries or other compensation for personal services actually rendered;

(3) makes any part of its services available on a preferential basis;

(4) makes any substantial purchase of securities or any other property for more than adequate consideration in money or money's worth;

(5) sells any substantial part of its securities or other property for less than adequate consideration in money or money's worth; or

(6) engages in any other transactions which result in a substantial diversion of its income or corpus.

Congress was also aware of another abuse which it attempted to remedy by legislation in 1950, namely, a number of foundations had accumulated substantial portions of their income, sometimes to the neglect of the tax-exempt purposes for which they were organized. The obvious consequence of unreasonable accumulation was that charity would not likely be the beneficiary of the accumulated

---

[11] Certain nonexempt trusts were also made subject to the prohibited "transactions" rule by the 1950 act. See section 681(b) of the 1954 code prior to its amendment in 1969.

[12] D. V. Moorehead, "The Tax Future of Private Foundations: Penalties for Self-Dealing and Jeopardy Investments," *New York University, 29th Annual Institute on Federal Taxation* (New York: Matthew Bender, 1971), p. 1872.

money—or, at the very least, beneficiary status would be unreasonably postponed.[13]

To remedy this problem the House proposed to subject to tax, with certain exceptions, that portion of the investment income of foundations which was not paid out on or before the fifteenth day of the third month following the close of the taxable year.[14]

Rejecting the House version as "too inflexible" and injurious to many worthwhile charitable projects, the Senate Finance Committee substituted in its place the requirement that information disclosing the extent of accumulations be made available to the public.[15]

The compromise reached in conference was enacted as part of the Revenue Act of 1950, and became sections 504 and 681(c) of the 1954 code. Those provisions denied exempt status to an otherwise qualifying organization for the year that its accumulated income was (1) unreasonable in amount or duration; (2) used to a substantial degree for purposes other than those constituting the basis for the organization's exemption; or (3) invested in such a manner as to jeopardize the carrying out of the functions constituting the basis for the organization's exemption.

The 1950 legislation was not intended only to correct abuses. It also was intended to eliminate the competitive advantages of exempt organizations over taxable businesses, and thus to assuage the complaints of those competing with charitable bodies.[16] To accomplish this objective Congress enacted a tax on the "unrelated business income" of certain exempt organizations and imposed a tax on "feeder organizations."[17]

---

[13] See House Report No. 2319, p. 40.

[14] H.R. 8920, as reported by the Ways and Means Committee, House Report No. 2319, pp. 40-41.

[15] Senate Report No. 2375, pp. 33-34.

[16] The following statements from ibid., pp. 28-29, describe the intention of Congress in enacting the unrelated business income provisions: "The problem at which the tax on unrelated business income is directed is primarily that of unfair competition. . . . It is not intended that the tax imposed on unrelated business income will have any effect on the tax-exempt status of any organization. An organization which is exempt prior to the enactment of this bill, if continuing the same activities, would still be exempt after this bill becomes law."

[17] The unrelated business income tax did not apply to a church, a convention or association of churches, or certain exempt trusts; section 511(a)(2)(A) of the 1954 code before amendment in 1969.

In connection with the "feeder organizations," Senate Report No. 2375, p. 35, and House Report No. 2319, p. 41, state: ". . . no organization operated primarily for the purpose of carrying on a trade or business . . . for profit shall be exempted [from tax] . . . merely on the grounds that all of its profits are payable to one or more organizations exempt from tax. . . . [S]uch an organization is not itself

The "unrelated business income" provisions, sections 511 to 514, imposed a tax on the net income in excess of $1,000 from any "unrelated trade or business regularly carried on."[18] The "feeder organization" provision, now section 502, flatly withdrew exempt status from organizations operated for the primary purpose of carrying on a trade or business, even if all their profits were payable to one or more tax-exempt organizations. The problems of construction and application of these provisions are not appropriate topics for this study. What is important, however, is that Congress expressed its concern in 1950 over the involvement of charitable and other tax-exempt organizations, including foundations, in business enterprises that were unrelated to the exempt purposes of those organizations.[19]

The Revenue Act of 1950 was an expression of congressional concern over the abuses of federal tax privileges accorded tax-exempt organizations and, in particular, charitable foundations. Foundations, however, came under scrutiny during the early 1950s for reasons other than those relating to the federal tax laws. In 1952 the climate of opinion in the United States was such that the criticism most frequently made against foundations, and the one urged with the greatest vehemence, was that foundations "supported or assisted persons, organizations, and projects which, if not subversive in the extreme sense of the word, tend to weaken or discredit the capitalistic system as it exists in the United States and to favor Marxist socialism."[20] In an effort to discover why the United States was confronted with Communist subversives and traitors, the House passed a resolution creating the Select Committee to Investigate and Study Edu-

---

carrying out an exempt purpose. Moreover, it obviously is in direct competition with other taxable business."

[18] Section 512(a).

[19] The House bill also contained a provision denying a charitable deduction if both of the following conditions existed: (1) the contributor, or members of his family, had voting control of the recipient organization; and (2) the contribution consisted of stock in a corporation in which the contributor, together with his family, controlled 50 percent or more or the stock, counting stock held by tax-exempt organizations which the family controlled.

The Senate Finance Committee rejected this provision on the ground that the donor or his family would be required to use the contributed property for charitable rather than personal purposes. Moreover, the Finance Committee felt that the tax avoidance considerations in situations described by the House bill would be outweighed by the fact that if these deductions were not allowed, still larger funds would be lost to private charity; Senate Report No. 2375, p. 39.

[20] U.S. Congress, House of Representatives, *Final Report of the Select Committee to Investigate Foundations and Other Organizations*, House Report No. 2514, 82d Congress, 2d session (1954), p. 9; hereinafter referred to as *Cox Committee Report*.

cational and Philanthropic Foundations and Other Comparable Organizations which Are Exempt from Federal Income Taxation.[21]

The chairman of this committee, Congressman Cox of Georgia, and its other members were authorized to conduct a complete investigation of philanthropic foundations in order to determine whether such organizations were using their resources for other than the purposes for which they were established and, in particular, to determine which foundations were using their resources for un-American and subversive activities.

Although the task was monumental, the Cox Committee was directed to report to the House no later than January 1, 1953. Despite this time limitation the committee managed to check into nearly all aspects of foundation operations. During the course of its investigation it sent questionnaires to more than 1,500 organizations, interviewed more than 200 persons, conducted hearings at which thirty-nine witnesses testified, including officers and trustees of the larger foundations, educators, and a group of Communist informers, and communicated by letter or telephone with approximately 200 more persons.

The final report described the growth, present and future needs, and role of foundations in the United States.[22] Although the investigation was engendered by a fear of left-wing subversive infiltration into foundations, the report was moderate in tone. In describing the role and the needs of foundations, it stated:

> While the important part they play and have played in palliative measures—that is, in relieving existing areas of suffering—must not be overlooked, their dominant and most significant function has been displayed in supplying the risk or venture capital expended in advancing the frontiers of knowledge. . . .
>
> . . . the present need for foundations is even greater than it has been in the past and . . . there is great likelihood that the need will prove an increasing one in the future. Despite the vast sums being poured by the Government into various fields formerly occupied by foundations and into fields in which the foundations and Government are cotenants or at least coadventurers, the need for the basic research so largely supplied and supported by the foundations continues to increase. Every new headland of human knowledge which is won opens up new vistas to be explored. As each mountain peak of discovery is scaled, vast new areas are laid open

---

[21] House Resolution 561, 82d Congress, 2d session (April 4, 1952).

[22] *Cox Committee Report.*

to exploration. . . . [T]here are ever-widening and length-
ening avenues of knowledge that require research and study
of the type and kind best furnished or assisted by foundations. The foundation, once considered a boon to society,
now seems to be a vital and essential factor in our progress.[23]

Mindful of its mandate to investigate criticisms directed against
foundations, the Cox Committee summarized its findings and conclusions with respect to these criticisms. After first noting that it
was allotted insufficient time for the magnitude of its task, the Cox
Committee then proceeded in its final report to deal with twelve
major questions which it believed were raised by the criticisms leveled
against foundations. These questions focused for the most part on
whether foundations had been involved in subversive activities or
channeled funds into the hands of subversive individuals and organizations. In response to this inquiry, it concluded as follows:

The committee believes that on balance the record of the
foundations is good. It believes that there was infiltration
and that judgments were made which, in the light of hindsight, were mistakes, but it also believes that many of these
mistakes were made without the knowledge of facts which,
while later obtainable, could not have been readily ascer-
tained at the time decisions were taken. It further believes
that the foundations are aware of the ever-present danger
and are exerting and will continue to exert diligence in avert-
ing further mistakes. . . . The committee does not want to
imply that errors of judgment constitute malfeasance.[24]

Although the Cox Committee concentrated on foundation involvement in subversive or left-wing activities, it also directed its
attention to the accountability of foundations to the public and to
the question of their possible abuse of the tax laws. With respect to
the problem of public accountability, it recommended that foundations be required to disclose certain information. As for tax abuses,
the Cox Committee concluded that such questions were matters for
the consideration of the Committee on Ways and Means and recommended that that committee re-examine pertinent tax laws "to the
end that they may be so drawn as to encourage the free-enterprise
system with its rewards from which private individuals may make
gifts to these meritorious institutions."[25]

---

[23] Ibid., pp. 3-5.
[24] Ibid., p. 8.
[25] Ibid., p. 13.

Aware of the limited time accorded to the Cox Committee within which to complete an extensive investigation and apparently still wary of foundation involvement in un-American and subversive activities, the House created another committee on July 27, 1953.[26] The Special Committee to Investigate Tax-Exempt Foundations and Comparable Organizations was authorized to conduct a complete investigation of educational and philanthropic foundations and other comparable organizations that were exempt from federal income tax in order to determine whether these organizations were using their resources not only for un-American and subversive activities, but also for political purposes, propaganda, or attempts to influence legislation.

Representative B. Carroll Reece, who had been one of the Cox Committee members and who had signed the unanimous Cox Committee Report with a reservation that there had been "insufficient time for the magnitude of its task," [27] had sponsored the House resolution and was appointed chairman of this new committee. The Reece Committee elicited testimony from twelve witnesses; of these witnesses, three were members of Reece's staff, and two were representatives of the Treasury Department. Of the remaining seven witnesses, five were general witnesses whose experience was entirely unrelated to foundations and their work.

> The thesis supported by the general witnesses and the staff testimony appeared to be that great changes had occurred in America in the direction of socialism and collectivism, with one witness holding that even the federal income tax was a socialist plot to destroy the government. These changes were aided, it was alleged, through a "diabolical conspiracy" of foundations and certain educational and research organizations.[28]

The only rebuttal permitted foundations was through the submission of written statements.

The final majority report [29] issued by the Reece Committee was signed by only three of the five committee members, and one of these

---

[26] House Resolution 217, 83rd Congress, 1st session (July 27, 1953).

[27] Cox Committee Report, p. 14.

[28] F. E. Andrews, Patman: Review and Assessment (New York: Foundation Center, 1968), p. 3.

[29] U.S. Congress, House of Representatives, Report of the Special Committee to Investigate Tax-Exempt Foundations and Comparable Organizations, House Report No. 2681, 83rd Congress, 2d session (1954); hereinafter cited as Reece Committee Report.

negated his signature by submitting a statement which concluded as follows: "Nothing has transpired in the proceedings of the present committee to cause me to alter or modify the views I expressed in the Cox Committee Report. I take this opportunity to again re-affirm them."[30]

A minority report was issued by the other two committee members which disagreed vehemently with the majority report. This minority report stated that the Reece Committee proceedings were conducted in a biased and unfair manner. Moreover, the statement of facts and opinion contained in the report were, according to minority members, either untrue on their face or were half-truths that were misleading. "The [majority] report outstrips the record in its bias, its prejudgment, and its obvious hatred for the object of its wrath— the principal private foundations of the Nation."[31]

Among the conclusions and recommendations of the majority report were a ten to twenty-five year limitation on the life of all foundations, required distribution of income including capital gains, and restrictions on corporation-controlled foundations. The majority report further recommended that the Internal Revenue Service increase its staff so as to supervise more closely foundation activity and suggested to the House Committee on Ways and Means that it consider the problem of prohibited transactions, political activity and lobbying, and foundation spending abroad.

Despite the criticisms leveled against foundations by the Reece Committee, no significant legislation was enacted which implemented its suggestions. Although the rest of the 1950s witnessed very little of the clamor generated by the Reece Committee, a renewed interest in foundations emerged during the early 1960s as the desire for more tax revenue increased.

In January 1962 the Select Committee on Small Business of the House of Representatives passed a resolution authorizing a study to be made of the impact of tax-exempt foundations on the American economy. The chairman of that committee, Wright Patman, undertook to conduct this investigation as an activity of Subcommittee Number 1 on Tax-Exempt Foundations. It was he who was the moving force behind the investigation. Throughout 1961 he made a number of speeches in the House in which he urged Congress to take another look at foundations and their activities because of the increase

---

[30] Statement of Honorable Angier L. Goodwin, quoted in Andrews, *Patman*, p. 4.
[31] "Minority Views," in *Reece Committee Report*, pp. 417, 429.

in their number and their concomitant gains in power and influence in American economic life. Patman's concern was focused on

> . . . first, foundation-controlled businesses competing with small businessmen; second, the economic effect of great amounts of wealth accumulating in privately controlled, tax-exempt foundations; third, the problem of control of that capital for an undetermined period—in some instances per-petuity—by a few individuals or their self-appointed succes-sors; and fourth, the foundations' power to interlock and knit together through investments, a network of commercial alliances, which assures harmonious action whenever they have a common interest.[32]

Approximately one year after the study was authorized by the House, Congressman Patman released an interim report to the Select Committee on Small Business which contained factual data and statistics on foundations as well as recommendations on how to curb their abuses.[33] It is interesting to note that this installment of the report, as well as some others which he submitted, represent Con-gressman Patman's findings, conclusions, and recommendations. These installment reports have been termed remarkable "because they are neither reports of a Committee to the House, nor of the subcommittee to the Committee, but merely reports of a chairman to his own subcommittee. In other words, they are only the opinion of a single individual."[34]

The first installment made recommendations dealing with foun-dation-related problems, most of which had been aired previously in the Cox or Reece Committee investigations. Mr. Patman's suggestions included the following: limiting to twenty-five years the existence of all foundations, setting up a regulatory agency for the supervision of tax-exempt foundations, prohibiting foundation involvement in business, and denying income tax deductions to donors with respect to contributions to controlled foundations until such gifts were used for charitable purposes.[35]

---

[32] *Congressional Record*, August 7, 1961, p. 14793.

[33] U.S. Congress, House of Representatives, Chairman's Report to Select Com-mittee on Small Business, *Tax-Exempt Foundations and Charitable Trusts: Their Impact on Our Economy*, first installment, 87th Congress, 2d session (December 31, 1962).

[34] R. K. Powell, "The Patman Report and the New Reporting Requirements," *New York University, 22nd Annual Institute on Federal Taxation* (New York: Matthew Bender, 1964), pp. 921, 922.

[35] Andrews, *Patman*, pp. 20-21.

Critics of the Patman investigation point to the ex parte nature of his reports and charge that they contain certain misstatements of facts. There were no hearings at which foundation representatives could defend their position. Furthermore, even other members of Subcommittee Number 1 did not participate in the investigation and these members objected vigorously to Mr. Patman's procedures.[36]

Despite the unorthodox procedures and ex parte nature of the investigation, Patman's critics do credit him with certain pluses—a focus on abuses attributable to foundations, a stimulation of public disclosure and fuller reporting, and a rendering of financial information.[37]

---

[36] Ibid., pp. 51-52.
[37] Fremont-Smith, *Foundations and Government*, pp. 371-372.

4

TREASURY DEPARTMENT REPORT ON PRIVATE FOUNDATIONS

In an effort to correct some of the tax abuses to which Patman, Reece, and Cox made reference, the Senate Finance Committee and the House Committee on Ways and Means asked the Treasury Department to prepare a special report on whether the 1950 amendments to the Internal Revenue Code were effective in eliminating these abuses and whether, in particular, correction by additional legislation might be needed.[1]

The Treasury Department conducted a special survey of approximately 1,300 private foundations—consisting of 100 percent of all foundations with assets of $10 million or more, 25 percent of those in the $1 million to $10 million category, 10 percent of those with assets of $100,000 to $1 million, and 5 percent of those with assets of $100,000 or less.

On February 2, 1965, the Treasury Department submitted its report to Congress. The Treasury report, while concluding that the preponderant number of private foundations perform their functions without tax abuse, also stated that six major problems existed among a minority which warranted additional corrective legislative measures. Before specifying the problems, however, the report first described the values associated with philanthropy and the part played by private foundations in realizing certain basic and important values. It then dealt with three general criticisms which had been directed at founda-

---

[1] The Revenue Act of 1964 contained provisions which differentiated between private foundations and publicly supported charitable organizations, a distinction expressing congressional sentiment at the time. For example, Congress increased from 20 to 30 percent of adjusted gross income the general limitation on the amount of deductible charitable contributions which individuals could make. However, it excluded from the increase donations to private foundations, continuing the 20 percent ceiling on such donations.

tions. The report concluded that the first of these, which was that the interposition of the foundation between the donor and active charitable pursuits entailed undue delay in the transfer of benefits to society, possessed "considerable force." However, it rejected as a viable solution any limitation on foundation life, suggesting instead legislative measures specifically designed to meet this problem.[2]

The second general criticism was that foundations were becoming a disproportionately large share of our national economy and were therefore eroding the tax base. In direct response to this charge, the Treasury report stated:

> While the available information is far from definitive, it suggests that, since 1950, foundation wealth has not grown appreciably faster than other segments of the economy which have substantial investments in common stocks. The existing restrictions on charitable deductions for contributions to foundations would seem to provide a significant restraint upon abnormal growth. Hence, there would appear to be little present factual basis for the assertion that foundation lives should be limited because foundation wealth has become disproportionate.[3]

The last general contention made by critics of private foundations was that they represented a dangerous concentration of uncontrolled economic and social power. The report concluded that, for the most part, the foundations were adequately dealing with that problem themselves.

The six major problems which occupied the attention of the Department of the Treasury were discussed under the following headings: (1) self-dealing, (2) delay in benefit to charity, (3) foundation involvement in business, (4) family use of foundations to control corporate and other property, (5) financial transactions unrelated to charitable functions, and (6) the broadening of foundation management.

Since the Treasury report laid the basis to a great extent for many of the provisions of the Tax Reform Act of 1969, this monograph will treat these problems in greater detail.

Self-Dealing

Self-dealing was by no means a new problem. Rather, as indicated earlier, it was a matter of great concern to Congress in 1950, when

---

[2] *Treasury Report*, p. 13.

[3] Ibid., pp. 13-14.

it passed the "prohibited transactions" rule which was re-enacted as section 503 of the Internal Revenue Code of 1954, before amendment in 1969. As a compromise between the bill proposed by the House of Representatives in 1950 and that advocated by the Senate, an arm's-length standard was adopted. In analyzing the self-dealing issue, the Treasury therefore had almost sixteen years of experience under an arm's length standard to help it determine whether such a rule was workable and effective in eliminating abuses.

Concluding in effect that the House of Representatives was correct in 1950, the Treasury report recommended that private foundations be prohibited from engaging in any transaction with the donor or parties related to the donor that involved the transfer or use of the foundation's assets. Under the Treasury report recommendation, a private foundation would be prohibited from engaging in the following activities with the donor or certain parties closely connected with the foundation: (1) lending any part of its income or corpus, (2) paying compensation (other than reasonable compensation for personal services), (3) making any of its services available on a preferential basis, (4) purchasing or leasing its property, and (5) selling or leasing its property.

Under the Treasury report, however, an exception would have been authorized to allow foundations to buy incidental supplies from the donor if he were in the business of supplying the kind of materials needed. Another exception would have been to allow a donor to make an interest-free loan to a foundation if such a loan were to be used for bona fide charitable purposes.

One of the most difficult problems, and one which was not dealt with by the Treasury report, concerns the types of sanctions to be imposed when a foundation engages in self-dealing. Under the 1950 legislation the sanction for a "prohibited transaction" was loss of tax exemption; however, the Treasury report did not indicate whether it favored this or a less severe sanction, and thus allowed the philosophy of "off with its head" to be perpetuated—but, as it turned out, not for long.

Delay in Benefit to Charity

Under the revenue laws effective in 1950, an immediate deduction was allowed for gifts to private foundations. In the case of contributions to operating foundations, an immediate deduction was considered appropriate by the Treasury report because the funds usually found their way into the charitable stream within a short

31

period after receipt by such foundations.[4] On the other hand, the Treasury concluded that contributions to some nonoperating foundations were not devoted to charitable activities and were not distributed to operating charities. Rather, the contributions were used and retained to generate income to be distributed to operating charities. In such a situation there is generally a significant lag between the time of the contribution, with its immediate effect on tax revenues attributable to the charitable deduction, and the time when the public benefits by having an equal amount of funds devoted to charitable activities.

Here again is another example of a problem which was dealt with in 1950, but not adequately in the opinion of the Treasury. In that year Congress enacted the predecessor of section 504 of the Internal Revenue Code of 1954 which established a rule of reasonableness in connection with the accumulation of income by foundations.

In view of this delay in benefit to charity, the Treasury recommended that all private, nonoperating foundations be required to expend the full amount of their current net income by the end of the year following the year such income is received. The term "income" was defined to include investment income such as rents, interest, dividends, and short-term capital gains. Under the Treasury proposal, long-term capital gains and contributions received by the foundations were not required to be distributed on a current basis, as defined.

In order to cover the situation where a foundation has very little income because of its investments in growth stock or assets, the Treasury report suggested that when a foundation's ordinary income fails to reach 3 percent (or some other reasonable percentage as determined by the secretary of the treasury) of the value of the foundation's assets, then an income equivalent was to be determined. This income equivalent was to be applied only against a foundation's investment assets and not against assets which the foundation used for its own charitable program.

---

[4] The Revenue Act of 1964 contained special rules for "unlimited gifts" to private operating foundations as defined in section 170(g)(2)(B) of the 1954 code before amendment in 1969. For the purpose of such rules and for the Treasury report's proposal, a private operating foundation was defined as a privately supported organization which has substantially more than one-half of its assets directly devoted to its active charitable activities and which must expend substantially all its income for charitable purposes on a current basis. Ibid., p. 23. A nonoperating foundation was a foundation that did not meet the definition of an operating foundation.

In addition to the above general requirements, the Treasury report proposed certain carry-over provisions and allowed five-year accumulations for a specified charitable purpose. Extensions of time for existing organizations to adjust their investments to meet the pay-out rule were also permitted; however, once again no sanctions or rules for enforcement were suggested by the Treasury.

Foundation Involvement in Business

The problem of foundation involvement in business is also not a new one. Congress recognized the problem in 1950 and proposed to solve it by the Revenue Act of that year, which for the first time subjected the unrelated business income of foundations and certain other exempt organizations to taxation at ordinary rates and removed the tax immunity enjoyed by "feeder" organizations.

The Treasury report concluded that serious difficulties arose from foundation commitment to business endeavors. Among these was that regular business enterprises often suffered serious competitive disadvantage. Furthermore, this situation presented opportunities for subtle and varied forms of self-dealing. Another consequence of foundation participation in business was that foundation management would tend to have less concern over charitable activities because of time-consuming concentration on commercial matters.

Recognizing that the unrelated business tax and the feeder provisions did not effectively deal with the problems presented by foundation commitment to business, the Treasury Department recommended the imposition of an absolute limit upon the extent of private foundations' participation in active business. It concluded that a foundation should be prohibited from owning 20 percent or more of the total combined voting power or 20 percent or more of the total value of the equity of a corporation conducting a business which is not substantially related to its exempt functions.[5]

Under the Treasury proposal, three carefully restricted forms of producing passive income were to be excluded from the definition of "business." Earning interest was not to be considered to constitute a business except in the case of active commercial lending or banking. Holding royalties and mineral production payments which were viewed as inactive investments were to be accorded similar

---

[5] A similar prohibition was recommended for ownership by a foundation of a 20 percent or larger interest in a partnership.

treatment. Finally, appropriate standards were to be developed to identify leases of real property which were of a clearly passive nature; rent arising from such leases was not deemed to be derived from the conduct of a business.

The Treasury report recommended that foundations should be given a reasonable period of time in which to reduce their unrelated business interests below the prescribed maximum limit. Moreover, the secretary of the treasury or his delegate was to be given power to extend the period for a limited additional time in appropriate cases.

Family Use of Foundations To Control Corporate and Other Property

A typical case of Treasury concern involved the owner of a closely held corporation who creates a foundation and then gives to that foundation a certain percentage of the stock of his company, thereby obtaining a current deduction for its fair market value. According to the Treasury report, the resulting relationships among the foundation, corporation, and donor have serious undesirable consequences calling for correction. Moreover, similar problems arise where a donor contributes an interest in an unincorporated business or an undivided interest in property in which he or related parties continue to have substantial rights because in all of these situations there is a substantial likelihood that private interests would be pursued at the expense of charity.

To remedy such a situation the Treasury Department recommended legislation that would in effect defer the charitable deduction to the donor until the charity really acquired something. In other words, the deduction was to be deferred until the stock was disposed of or until the donor ceased to have a controlling interest in the company. Specifically, under this recommendation, if the donor and related parties continue to maintain control of a business or other property after contributing an interest in it to a private foundation, no income tax deduction would be permitted for the gift until (1) the foundation disposed of the contributed assets; (2) the foundation devoted the property to active charitable operations; or (3) the donor no longer controlled the business or property.

The Treasury recommended as a correlative provision that transfers of such an interest made at or before death were to be treated as incomplete transfers for estate tax purposes unless one of the foregoing three conditions was fulfilled within a specified period after the donor's death. For purposes of this rule, if the donor and related parties owned 20 percent of the voting power of a corporation or a 20 percent interest in an unincorporated business or property, control would have been presumed to exist. However, this presumption could have been rebutted by showing that a particular interest did not constitute control.

The Treasury also considered another recommendation to resolve the problem of the use of foundations to control corporate and other property. This recommendation would have postponed the donor's deduction only when he and related parties controlled the business or other property and, in addition, when they exercised substantial influence over the foundation to which the contribution was made. The effect of this rule was to permit an immediate deduction to a donor who transferred control of property to a foundation over which he did not have substantial influence. The advantage of this alternative recommendation is that immediate deductions were to be allowed in a limited number of situations in which gifts of controlled property to private foundations produced clear charitable benefits and were not accompanied by abuses. Nevertheless, two rather grave difficulties were found by the Treasury to inhere in this alternative recommendation.

The first difficulty is over a satisfactory definition of "substantial donor influence." The second problem results from the restriction of the controlled property rule to situations in which the recipient foundation is under donor influence. The Treasury recognized that the donor's continuing power over his corporation exists whether or not the foundation to which he gives the stock is subject to his influence. Therefore, the result would be that charity would benefit only infrequently from the gift of controlled corporation stock.

After presenting these two alternative solutions to the problem of the family use of foundations for control of corporations and other property, the Treasury left it to Congress to determine which would be the better and more workable one.

Financial Transactions Unrelated to Charitable Functions

Although the Treasury report recognized that foundations must necessarily engage in many transactions connected with the investment of their funds, it also concluded that unrestricted foundation participation in three classes of financial activities could produce unfortunate results. These three classes are borrowing, lending, and trading and speculation by foundations.

The Treasury believed that foundation borrowing for investment could cause damage because in many cases it is merely a way of deflecting to the personal benefit of private parties a portion of the advantage which tax exemption intended to produce for charity. In order to prevent this result the Treasury report recommended the prohibition of all borrowing by private foundations for investment purposes except where the objective is to carry on exempt functions.

The second class of financial activities subjected to Treasury scrutiny was foundation lending. Many private foundations had used their funds to make loans which were not secured by mortgages and were not evidenced by government or other bonds. When a private foundation engaged in privately motivated lending, charity would have been the ultimate sufferer. Since the safety of the obligation was not among the primary considerations in making a loan, foundations sometimes took unusual and unnecessary risks. In order to remedy the situation the Treasury recommended confinement of foundation loans to categories that were clearly necessary, safe, and appropriate for charitable fiduciaries.

The Treasury also concluded that there were inherent dangers in securities trading and speculative investments. The first and most obvious danger is that either practice, when compared to long-term, prudently selected investments, necessarily entails greater risk of loss. The argument continues that assets which have been committed to charity should not be subject to such risk. Another danger is that foundation trustees or directors could become so involved in playing the markets that they would not spend enough time in looking after the interests of charity.

The efforts of the speculator or the trader, according to the Treasury report, were intrinsically inconsistent with the proper management of the affairs of the charitable foundation. Therefore, the report recommended that private foundations be directly prohibited from participating in any kind of trading or speculation with any of their assets, whether derived from corpus or from income.

Broadening of Foundation Management

While recognizing that a donor might provide unique direction to a foundation during its formative years, the Treasury felt that this advantage tends to diminish with time and perhaps disappear altogether following the donor's death. Moreover, influence by the donor or his family sometimes fosters narrowness of view and inflexibility in foundation management. As a consequence, the Treasury recommended an approach that proposed to broaden the base of foundation management after the first twenty-five years of a founda-

36

tion's life. After that period the donor and related parties were not to constitute more than 25 percent of the foundation's governing body.

The Treasury also made recommendations to deal with what were described as "additional problems." These recommendations were: (1) deductions for donations of certain classes of unproductive property were to be postponed until the assets were either made productive, disposed of, or applied to charitable uses; (2) the amount of the deduction for donations to foundations was to be reduced by any amounts of income they would have generated to the donor if they had been sold rather than donated; (3) technical changes were to be made in certain provisions of the estate tax laws which gave unfair advantage to decedents who made contributions to foundations; and (4) more appropriate sanctions for failure to file information returns were to be enacted.

As will be noted, the Treasury report did not deal with many foundation-related problems that could be considered new. Most of these problems existed in 1950 when remedial action on some of them was taken by Congress. Indeed, many of the recommendations of the Treasury report were the same proposed and adopted by the House of Representatives in 1950.

Notwithstanding any criticism that might be directed at some of the substantive content of the Treasury report and the statistical sampling procedures which underpinned its findings, the report is a painstakingly prepared, dispassionate, and reasoned study that played a very important role in 1969 in reforming the internal revenue laws with respect to private foundations. Indeed, many of its recommendations, somewhat modified, were accepted and adopted by Congress in the Tax Reform Act of 1969.

5

COMMISSION ON
FOUNDATIONS AND
PRIVATE PHILANTHROPY

One of the most recent important studies of foundations was undertaken by the Commission on Foundations and Private Philanthropy. Late in 1968, John D. Rockefeller III, sensing the rising tide of antagonism and resentment towards foundations, was the motivating force behind a series of meetings which focused on two principal questions: (1) Is it possible to secure an independent appraisal of American philanthropy? and (2) What should be the long-range role of philanthropy and foundations in American life? At the suggestion of Alan Pifer, president of the Carnegie Corporation, an independent commission was formed to study all relevant matters bearing on foundations and private philanthropy and to deliver a report containing appropriate long-range policy recommendations. In February 1969, Mr. Rockefeller invited Peter G. Peterson to form the proposed commission, to be composed of a group of private citizens. The main criteria for choosing the members and staff were to safeguard the independence of the commission and have it embrace the broadest possible range of representative viewpoints. The time was indeed ripe for such a commission, for in early 1969 both old and familiar charges, as well as some new ones, were being leveled against foundations.

The Peterson Commission, as it became known, produced a report that evaluated the role of philanthropy and foundations in American society, commented upon the abuses prevalent among some foundations, and made recommendations concerning the future of foundations in the American way of life.[1]

---

[1] *Foundations, Private Giving, and Public Policy: Report and Recommendations of the Commission on Foundations and Private Philanthropy* (Chicago: University of Chicago Press, 1970); hereinafter cited as *Peterson Commission Report.*

The survey method employed by the commission has been criticized as not representative. These critics argue that the Peterson Commission statistics are therefore shaky and uncertain. However, even the critics believe that the Peterson Commission report identifies several very relevant issues regarding foundations and American philanthropy. According to one critic: "It is a commentary on the extent of the void of pertinent information about philanthropy that the Commission's data, wobbly as it is, is still the best that we have on several important aspects." [2]

The lack of data on foundations is probably as much attributable to the foundations themselves as to anyone else. Naturally, lack of information can create misconceptions. One of the greatest misconceptions about foundations—which was pointed out by the Peterson Commission report—was the widespread belief at the time of the passage of the Tax Reform Act of 1969 that foundations have a "monolithic sameness." [3]

As the Peterson Commission report indicates, foundations vary in size from those with no endowments and only a few thousand dollars in annual grants to the other end of the scale where the measurement is approximately $3 billion in assets and annual grants of approximately $200 million. Other differences among foundations are that some are donor controlled while others are independent of the donor. Moreover, contributions may be made to foundations by one person, a company, or a number of unrelated persons; and they may be made only upon one occasion rather than on a regularly recurring basis.

In order to insure that misunderstandings and misconceptions would not recur, the Peterson Commission report recommended full and early disclosure and public reporting of foundation activities. According to the report, public reporting not only serves the public's right to know, but can also be one of the most powerful means of achieving fuller accountability to the public. The argument is that an informed and understanding public will weed out only the bad and not the good. Foundations themselves should want no less, for otherwise their existence is threatened and the benefits flowing from their activities could come to a halt.

The Peterson Commission report made recommendations to foundations and to the government in an effort to insure that Amer-

---

[2] W. A. Nielsen, "The Peterson Commission Report: A Review, a Critical Analysis, and a Projection," N.Y.U. Conference on Charitable Foundations, vol. 10, pp. 1, 3.

[3] Peterson Commission Report, p. 47.

ican philanthropy and American philanthropic foundations would continue to make unique contributions to the general welfare. These recommendations were guided by certain principles. For example, the commission did not approve of voluntary self-control in the specific financial realm in which foundations have abused their tax-exempt privilege, either by using their resources for private gain or for purposes that are not charitable. In line with this principle, the Peterson Commission therefore strongly recommended that there be government supervision of foundations in those financial areas where the donors or certain related persons could take advantage of or corrupt the integrity of the tax system.

Another guiding principle was that government regulation of foundation grant programs should not be punitive and a form of indirect control over every phase of foundation life. One of the greatest sources of foundation utility, according to the report, is its freedom of decision in regard to the grants it makes. Therefore, the report argues it is up to the foundations to use their freedom in a responsible manner. This implies that foundation trustees and managers must become completely immersed in the work of their foundations.

An addendum to the last stated principle is the idea that society has a critical need for tax-supported projects, and therefore the billions of dollars of tax-exempt funds are expected to make a full contribution to society. Government regulation is necessary but not to the extent that it impairs foundation willingness to recognize and accept a deep-rooted responsibility to invest assets productively.

The Peterson Commission report, as is evidenced from the foregoing, does not take an all-or-nothing approach to the problems existing in the foundation world. Instead, it tries to combine government supervision in some areas with private self-direction in others. It also puts the spotlight on another very important and often overlooked idea, that is, that the needs of philanthropy and charitable organizations cannot and should not be determined solely by reference to the tax laws. Rather, decisions affecting charitable organizations, even though they are embedded in the tax law, should reflect the broadest considerations of public policy. Therefore, the Peterson Commission recommended the creation of an advisory board on philanthropic policy which would assure that the needs and problems of philanthropy would be effectively articulated within the government.

Although the final report of the Peterson Commission was published after the passage of the Tax Reform Act of 1969, the commission did contribute to the legislative deliberations of 1969. It was asked to present its findings and recommendations to Congress and to address itself specifically to the questions which Congress was debating at the time. No doubt, the Peterson Commission report had its impact on the Tax Reform Act of 1969 and will also have an important bearing on future legislation affecting tax-exempt foundations.

6
THE TAX REFORM
ACT OF 1969

In direct contrast to its previous history of acting slowly and perhaps not effectively, Congress decided in 1969 to move on reported foundation abuses, and to move swiftly. Indeed, in the opinion of some critics, Congress acted much too swiftly, even allowing emotion to prevail over reason to some degree.

What spurred Congress to undertake a monumental revision of the tax law with respect to foundations? For one thing, the American public was said to be growing increasingly unhappy over inequities in the tax burden. Also, certain events triggered a change in congressional attitude toward tax reform with respect to foundations. For example, the belief that foundation money had been used to help register voters in specified cities or counties and so caused or prevented the election of certain candidates surely did nothing to inspire congressional love of foundations. In particular, the Ford Foundation authorized a grant to the Congress of Racial Equality (CORE). This grant was said to have been used to widen voter registration in a Cleveland slum area and was alleged to have aided the election of Carl B. Stokes as mayor in November 1967 and to have contributed to the defeat of Mr. Taft. The criticism directed at the CORE grant was that the Ford Foundation, by selecting the exact location where money was to be spent for voter registration, influenced the election results.[1]

Newspaper accounts that some officials had accepted important government positions with the understanding that they would be reemployed by foundations upon their departure from office contributed to congressional suspicion that foundations somehow could find ways to unduly influence governmental decisions.

---

[1] *House Hearings*, p. 411.

At about this stage Senator John J. Williams of Delaware introduced Senate Bill 2075 which was designed to become part of the Federal Unemployment Tax Bill that had already passed the House of Representatives.[2] The objective of the Williams bill was to prevent "improper transactions" between government officials and the private sector. No doubt the allegations asserted against Mr. Justice Fortas and Mr. Justice Douglas regarding their connections with certain foundations precipitated congressional concern over the relationships between government officials and private foundations. In fact, in introducing the bill, Senator Williams referred specifically to the activities of the Wolfson Foundation and its relation to Mr. Justice Fortas.

Some of the provisions of the Williams bill would have barred all payments to government officials by foundations or the beneficiaries of foundation grants, and furthermore would have proscribed all payments by foundations to government officials for a period of two years after government service.

The basic purposes of the Williams bill—to deny to private foundations the right to expend funds so as to exert improper influence on government decisions and to prevent government officials from receiving benefits inconsistent with their obligations to government— were supported by most private foundations. Nonetheless, the sweeping provisions of the bill met with considerable criticism. Senator Williams withdrew his bill but only upon the reassurance that a provision with the same objectives of the Williams bill would be introduced as part of the tax reform package on private foundations.[3]

Another spark lighting a fire under Congress in 1969 was wrapped up in the grants for "travel and study" to several members of Senator Robert Kennedy's campaign staff following the senator's assassination. Certain members of Congress were outraged at these grants because they could not see any intellectual benefit flowing from them.

The foregoing were bound to have an emotional effect on the deliberative process of reforming the taxing statute. However, real abuses did exist that needed attention. They have been chronicled earlier in this monograph, but at the risk of some repetition there are five basic areas of abuse of the tax-exemption privilege that may be listed now and against which the provisions of the Tax Reform Act of 1969 were directed: (1) self-dealing between substantial contributors and their foundations, (2) the failure to distribute founda-

---

[2] H.R. 9951, 91st Congress, 1st session (1969).
[3] *Congressional Record*, July 30, 1969, p. S. 21402-21406.

tion income to charities, (3) foundation ownership and control of private businesses, (4) speculation jeopardizing foundation investments, and (5) the use of foundation money for programs or activities not within the scope of the tax-exemption provisions.

Since this part of tax reform in 1969 was made applicable only to "private foundations," Congress was required to define that term. The definition now appears in section 509(a) of the Internal Revenue Code of 1954.

The statutory definition of "private foundation" reflects an underlying congressional philosophy which turns upon a very crucial distinction between organizations that are privately financed and those that depend upon the public for their support. In the latter case, the organization is subject to the discipline of public opinion. If it misbehaves, misuses its capital, or engages in questionable practices, the public will presumably learn about it and, by the simple expedient of cutting off contributions, correct that which has become offensive.

On the other hand, the institution that is privately financed is subject to no such corrective influence and therefore must be regulated in some other way. In an effort to prevent such an organization from escaping private foundation status, the statutory approach adopted in section 509(a) is to define what a private foundation is not, rather than what it is.

A private foundation [4] is defined as any domestic or foreign organization described in section 501(c)(3) other than the following:

(1) An organization described in section 170(b)(1)(A)(i) through (vi) (this includes a church or convention or association of churches, an educational institution having a regular faculty, curriculum, and enrolled student body, a hospital, a governmental unit, and any organization which normally receives a substantial part of its support from the general public or from a governmental unit);

(2) An organization which normally receives not more than one-third of its support from gross investment income (such as interest, dividends, rents, et cetera) and normally receives more than one-third of its support from persons other than "disqualified persons," [5] from governmental units, or from organizations described in section 170(b)(1)(A)(i) through (vi), from any com-

---

[4] Hereinafter the term "private foundation" will refer only to those organizations meeting the definition set out in section 509(a), unless otherwise indicated.

[5] The term "disqualified person" is defined in section 4946(a). See discussion below, pages 53-55, and footnotes 23-28, this chapter.

bination of gifts, grants, contributions, or membership fees, and gross receipts from admissions, performance of services, or furnishing facilities;

(3) An organization organized and operated exclusively for the benefit of, to perform the functions of, or to carry out the purposes of one or more organizations described in (1) and (2) above, and supervised, controlled, or operated by or in connection with such organizations;[6] and

(4) An organization organized and operated exclusively for public safety.[7]

The determination whether an organization is a private foundation under section 509(a) is extremely complex, as is evidenced by regulations issued under that section. Although the intricacies of these regulations are not an appropriate topic for this study, one problem which did surface in them was that some charitable organizations may not have possessed the records necessary to make the computations called for.[8]

Excise Taxes Imposed by Chapter 42

A private foundation as defined in section 509(a) is subject to certain excise taxes in chapter 42 of the Internal Revenue Code of 1954.[9] Only one of these excise taxes, namely, the 4 percent excise tax on net investment income, is imposed regardless of whether the private foundation engages or fails to engage in certain kinds of activity. The remaining taxes are imposed only if the private foundation engages in proscribed activity or fails to engage in certain required activity.

Critics and advocates of the new statutory controls on private foundations will probably agree on at least one point, namely, that

---

[6] Section 509(a)(3) organizations are subject therefore to the safeguards implicit in being controlled, operated or supervised by other publicly supported organizations, rather than being subject directly to public scrutiny.

[7] Since contributions to institutions organized and operated exclusively for public safety are not deductible under section 170, the potential for abuse by such organizations was lacking and, accordingly, Congress classified them as nonprivate foundations.

[8] For an excellent discussion of these regulations as first proposed under the private foundation provisions, see C. C. Hauser, "How Infirm a Foundation," *Taxes*, vol. 49 (December 1971), p. 49.

[9] Certain nonexempt trusts having charitable beneficiaries are also subject to some or all of the rules established in chapter 42; see section 4947(a).

private foundation rules constitute a complicated piece of legislation. One commentator noted that the act as it relates to foundations can aptly be referred to as the "Lawyers' and Accountants' Relief Act."[10] There has been an enormous—if not unprecedented—amount of cooperation and communication between the private sector, the Internal Revenue Service, and the Department of the Treasury in the development and promulgation of regulations interpreting the new law. During this period, which has already lasted over four full years, it is not unlikely that some foundations may tend to overreact or act only with excessive caution. Thus, in analyzing the impact of the new law on the role of private foundations, one must be careful to differentiate the long-term effect from the short-term impact, the latter being attributable to a large extent to the uncertainty of interpretation attending any new legislation.

Excise Tax on Net Investment Income—Section 4940

Section 4940 imposes an annual 4 percent excise tax on the net investment income of a private foundation. Net investment income is the amount by which the sum of gross investment income[11] and net capital gains exceeds the ordinary and necessary expenses paid or incurred for the production or collection of gross investment income or for the management, conservation, or maintenance of property held for the production of such income.[12]

Section 4940 creates very few technical problems of interpretation. However, one of the questions not answered by the statute but addressed by the regulations is the treatment of distributions to private foundations from charitable trusts described in section 4947 (a)(1) or (2). In brief, are the distributions to be treated as gifts, or must they be included as investment income in the hands of the private foundation to the extent that they represent in the hands of the trust the categories of income specifically set forth in section

---

[10] K. C. Eliasberg, "New Law Threatens Private Foundations: An Analysis of the New Restrictions," *Journal of Taxation*, vol. 32 (1970), p. 156.

[11] Gross investment income is defined by section 4940(c)(2) as the gross amount of income from interest, dividends, rents, and royalties, but not including such income subject to the tax imposed by section 511 on unrelated business income.

[12] In determining the amount of net capital gains, the basis of property held by a private foundation on December 31, 1969, and continuously thereafter to the date of its disposition is deemed not to be less than its fair market value on that date. Moreover, losses from sales or other dispositions are allowed only to the extent of gains from these transactions, and no capital loss carry-overs are allowable.

4940(c)(2)? Treasury Department Regulation section 53.4940-1(d)(2) provides a solution to this problem by stating that the character of the distribution in the hands of the trust is not to be retained by the private foundation except for distributions from split-interest trusts of income attributable to transfers in trust after May 26, 1969.[13]

The result of this rule is that distributions of income from wholly charitable trusts would be taxed under section 4940 only at the trust level and not at the level of the private foundation. In contrast, split-interest trusts are not themselves subject to section 4940 so that such tax is imposed at the private foundation level only in the case of income attributable to transfers in trust after May 26, 1969.

As indicated earlier, the other chapter 42 taxes are imposed only if a foundation engages in certain proscribed activities. Only the private foundation can bring upon itself the burden of these taxes, although sometimes unintentionally. In this respect the section 4940 tax is dissimilar from the other chapter 42 taxes and from the tax on unrelated business income provided in sections 511 through 514.

The unrelated business income tax is imposed upon section 501(c)(3) organizations only if they have "unrelated business taxable income." [14] Therefore, both the tax on unrelated business income and the taxes described in sections 4941 through 4945 are in the nature of penalties, the imposition of which is triggered by the organization itself.

On the other hand, section 4940, which imposes a tax on net investment income, is not triggered by any act or omission on the part of a private foundation. However, when section 4940 tax is assessed, it serves to reduce the funds that would be otherwise available for distribution to charity. In contrast, the other chapter 42 penalty taxes do not reduce the level of charitable distributions which private foundations are required to make.

---

[13] A split-interest trust, as defined by section 4947(a)(2), is one that is not exempt from tax under section 501(a), not all of the unexpired interests in which are devoted to one or more charitable, educational or other similar purposes and which has amounts in trust for which a charitable contribution deduction was allowed under any of several provisions.

[14] The term "unrelated business taxable income" means the gross income derived by any organization from any unrelated trade or business regularly carried on by it less deductions for expenses directly connected with the carrying on of such trade or business. The term "unrelated trade or business" means any trade or business, the conduct of which is not substantially related to the exercise or performance by an organization of its charitable, educational or other purpose or function constituting the basis for its exemption.

One of the most striking features of section 4940 is that it breaks a tradition extending over half a century—a tradition that exempts charitable organizations from federal taxation. As originally enacted by the House of Representatives, a 7½ percent income tax would have been imposed on the investment income of private foundations.[15] The reasons advanced for this tax are twofold: (1) since the benefits of government are available to all, its costs should be borne, at least to some extent, by all those with the ability to pay, including private foundations; and (2) private foundations should help support the administrative measures that will guarantee that they use their funds for charitable purposes.[16]

When the bill reached the Senate, the Committee on Finance substituted a user fee measured as a percentage of assets. The proposal, as amended on the Senate floor, established a fee that was to have been one-fifth of 1 percent of the value of the marketable assets of private foundations, but in no event less than $100. While agreeing with the House as to the need for supervision of private foundations, the Committee on Finance believed that it was important to distinguish between the need for a "user charge" and any withdrawal of the income tax exemption of such organizations. As it stated in its report:

> It . . . is appropriate to continue income tax exemption . . . for these organizations without any reduction in any manner in this tax-exempt status. Because of this it believes it is more appropriate to cast this audit fee in the form of a charge measured by the value of the assets to be supervised and examined rather than in the form of a charge on income which some, however inappropriately, might view as a beginning in the removal of income tax exemption.
>
> Accordingly, the committee determined to impose an annual tax as a percentage (subject to a minimum) of the noncharitable assets of the foundation.
>
> The committee views this tax as a supervisory fee and as an indication of the amount of funds needed by the Internal Revenue Service for proper administration of the Internal Revenue Code provisions relating to private foundations and other exempt organizations.[17]

As is apt to occur in situations such as this, the conferees tried to compromise the divergent approaches adopted by the House and

---

[15] H.R. 13270 (1969).

[16] House Report No. 91-413, 91st Congress, 2d session (1969), p. 19.

[17] Senate Report No. 91-552, 91st Congress, 1st session (1969), p. 27.

Senate. The result was the 4 percent excise tax imposed by section 4940 on the net investment income of private foundations. The staff of the Joint Committee explained the reasons underlying this excise tax as follows:

The Congress has concluded that private foundations should share some of the burden of paying the cost of government, especially for more extensive and vigorous enforcement of the tax laws relating to exempt organizations. However, the Congress believes that private foundations should continue to be exempt from income tax. Accordingly, the Act casts the charge or audit fee for private foundations in the form of an excise tax with respect to the carrying on of the organization's activities, rather than as a [income] tax under chapter 1 of the Internal Revenue Code.[18]

Regardless of what label is attached to the tax imposed by section 4940, it is a tax on the investment *income* of foundations. Saying that private foundations "should continue to be exempt from income tax" does not change this fact. Thus, it appears that the Senate sacrificed an important principle in accepting the compromise achieved by the conference committee.

At this point, it might be useful to consider that the Peterson Commission also endorsed the imposition of an audit fee on foundations for a three-year period to cover the costs of stepped-up regulatory activity directed at determining the level and nature of foundation abuses, bolstering public confidence in the legality of their activities, and assessing the need for future regulatory activity on the basis of concrete facts rather than isolated incidents. The commission, however, opposed the 4 percent tax on investment income on the ground that it could discourage the establishment of new foundations. In its final report, the commission stated:

The initial tax rate set by the law is low. Yet it creates a bad precedent, since the rate could easily be increased in a moment of disfavor and could be broadened to include other charitable organizations. It seems inconsistent and counterproductive to encourage giving to charitable organizations and then to impose a tax on foundation income which inevitably reduces the flow of funds to these organizations by diminishing the amount available for foundation grants. The impact of the new tax will be felt by potential grant recipients—primarily charitable organizations—far more

---

[18] *General Explanation of the Tax Reform Act of 1969*, prepared by the staff of the Joint Committee on Internal Revenue Taxation, December 3, 1970, p. 29.

than by foundations themselves. Moreover, because the tax flows into general government funds and is not earmarked for improved regulation of foundations, it cannot be justified as a regulatory instrument.[19]

One cannot quarrel with the proposition that private foundations should contribute to the support of administrative measures necessary to insure that their funds will be used for charitable purposes. However, section 4940—inadvertently or otherwise—reflects a congressional judgment that foundations should share some of the general expenses of government. In brief, no matter how one looks at it, it is a general revenue-producing measure. No solace can be taken from the fact that some of the revenue raised by section 4940 may be used for the enforcement of the tax laws relating to exempt organizations, for there remains the nagging question of how to justify the fact that private foundations will support efforts to determine compliance with the statute in the case of country clubs and mutual ditch companies—organizations that are also exempt from taxation. Moreover, assuming a justification is found, there is no assurance that such revenue will be used for the Internal Revenue Service audit of exempt organizations because there is no earmarking of the funds for this purpose. Finally, the monies collected apparently will produce substantially more revenues than are needed to fund the various programs of the Internal Revenue Service dealing with exempt organizations.

The appropriation requests for fiscal year 1972 revealed that the 4 percent tax on net investment income was expected to yield $35 million in revenue for that year. This same appropriation request indicated that $19.3 million was required to fund the Internal Revenue Service programs relating to exempt organizations. Included in this estimate was the base, that is, the costs of these programs built up over the years as well as the expanded operation called for by the Tax Reform Act for 1972 and later years.

Interestingly, while the revenue expected to be produced by the 4 percent excise tax for fiscal year 1973 was not increased, the appropriation request indicated that only $18.1 million, or $1.2 million less than for fiscal year 1972, would be needed to fund the service's exempt organization programs for fiscal year 1973.

One can speculate as to the reasons for this decrease in funding —such as the fact that compliance by exempt organizations may be far better than one would have believed from the debate preceding the 1969 act. Or perhaps the fiscal year 1972 expected costs were

---

[19] *Peterson Commission Report*, p. 167.

inflated beyond actual need. Or, more charitably, perhaps the Treasury was able to sharpen its request on the basis of a year's experience.

Speculation aside, several conclusions can be validly drawn from the appropriation requests for both fiscal years 1972 and 1973. First of all, it is readily apparent that the estimated fiscal year 1972 revenue receipts derived from the 4 percent tax almost doubled the funds that were needed by the Internal Revenue Service to cover all costs associated with exempt organizations. The projections for fiscal year 1973 also indicated that only approximately one-half of the projected revenue for that year would be needed to fund the costs associated with exempt organization programs. Thus, the remaining half of the funds raised by the tax (approximately $16.9 million) which would otherwise be used for charitable purposes is being used for general governmental purposes. Can this result be called the government's gain or can it be more appropriately labeled charity's loss?

The primary objection to section 4940 is philosophical: what justification can exist for imposing a tax on the investment income of a private foundation if the other foundation provisions are designed to insure that foundation funds will be used solely for charity? Viewed in this light, there is no reason to decrease the amount of funds available for charitable endeavors through the imposition of a tax on the investment income of private foundations.

A viable alternative to the section 4940 tax would be a tax measured by the value of a private foundation's assets, rather than one imposed upon its net investment income. Such a tax would be compatible with the goal of encouraging the current production of more income for current distribution to charitable beneficiaries. Further, it would be consistent with the half-century tradition of extending to private foundations the privilege of exemption from federal income taxation. Finally, it would continue to provide the funds for whatever amount of reasonable regulation these organizations would seem to need.

Prohibition against Self-Dealing—Section 4941

Section 4941, which replaces section 503 as it related to foundations, imposes a graduated series of sanctions on the self-dealer and, in certain instances, on a foundation manager with respect to each act of self-dealing between a foundation and a disqualified person. Section 4941(d) defines the term self-dealing as any direct or indirect

(1) sale or exchange, or leasing, of property between a private foundation and a disqualified person;

(2) lending of money or other extension of credit between a private foundation and a disqualified person;

(3) furnishing of goods, services, or facilities between a private foundation and a disqualified person;

(4) payment of compensation (or payment or reimbursement of expenses) by a private foundation to a disqualified person;

(5) transfer to, or use by or for the benefit of, a disqualified person of the income or assets of a private foundation; and

(6) with certain exceptions, any agreement by a private foundation to make any payment of money or other property to a government official other than an agreement to employ such individual after completion of his government service if such individual is terminating his government service within a ninety-day period.

As first proposed, the regulations under section 4941 indicated that an act of self-dealing would include a transaction between a private foundation and a disqualified person even though the status of the disqualified person arises only as a result of such transaction. The final regulations have, however, adopted a more sound and equitable rule by specifically stating that the term "self-dealing" does not include a transaction between a disqualified person and a private foundation where the disqualified person status arises only as a result of such transaction.[20]

Although the statute proscribes both direct and indirect acts of self-dealing, no satisfactory definition of what the phrase "indirect act of self-dealing" encompasses is available. Neither the committee reports nor the regulations define the term "indirect." Treasury Department Regulation section 53.4941(d)-1(b) merely describes six categories of transactions which are not considered as indirect acts of self-dealing, and thus it is extremely difficult to ascertain whether certain acts not falling within these categories would constitute "indirect" acts of self-dealing.

The statute provides that any sale of property between a private foundation and a disqualified person is an act of self-dealing, and the regulations make it clear that this includes the sale of incidental supplies by a disqualified person to a private foundation regardless of the amount paid by the foundation for the supplies.[21] However,

---

[20] Treasury Department Regulation section 53.4941(d)-1(a). (Hereinafter all regulations cited are Treasury Department regulations, unless otherwise stated.)
[21] Reg. section 53.4941(d)-2(a)(1).

Treasury Regulation section 53.4941(d)-2(d)(2) allows a private foundation to furnish goods, services or facilities to a foundation manager in recognition of his services as foundation manager, or to another employee in recognition of his services in such capacity, if the value of such furnishing is reasonable and necessary to the performance of his tasks in carrying out the foundation's exempt purposes and, taken in conjunction with any other payment of compensation or payment or reimbursement of expenses to him by the foundation, is not excessive. This exception applies whether or not the furnishing of goods, facilities or services is includible as compensation in the gross income of the foundation manager or other employee.

As one commentator observed shortly after regulations were first proposed under section 4941, this provision may "undoubtedly prove to be the greatest trap for the unwary of all the private foundation provisions." [22]

Since self-dealing can occur only where a "disqualified person" is present, it is necessary to understand the scope of the term. Section 4946 defines a "disqualified person" as a person who is (1) a substantial contributor [23] to the foundation; (2) a foundation manager; [24] (3) a person who owns more than 20 percent of a corporation, partnership, trust, or unincorporated enterprise which is itself a substantial contributor; (4) a member of the family of any individual in the first three categories; [25] (5) a corporation, partnership, trust, or estate in which any or all such persons in the first four categories own or hold more than 35 percent of the voting power, profits interest, or beneficial interest; [26] (6) for purposes of section 4943 only, certain

---

[22] Hauser, "How Infirm a Foundation," p. 759.

[23] A substantial contributor means an individual, corporation or other entity which has contributed or bequeathed in the aggregate more than $5,000, if such amount is more than 2 percent of the total contributions and bequests received by the foundation before the close of the taxable year in which a contribution or bequest is received by the foundation from such person; Reg. section 1.507-6(a)(1). In the case of a trust, the term also means the creator of a trust. Moreover, once a person is a substantial contributor, he will be treated as such forever after; Reg. section 1.507-6(b)(1).

[24] Section 4946(b) states that a "foundation manager" means, with respect to a private foundation, an officer, director, trustee, or other person having powers or responsibilities similar to those of officers, directors, or trustees. Moreover, that term means, with respect to any act or failure to act, the employees of the foundation having authority or responsibility with respect to such act or failure to act.

[25] Section 4946(d) defines "members of a family" of an individual as including only his spouse, ancestors, lineal descendants, and spouses of lineal descendants.

[26] Section 4946(a)(1)(E) through (G).

other private foundations;[27] and (7) for purposes of section 4941 only, a government official.[28]

The classification of a government official as a disqualified person fulfills the promise to Senator Williams to include as part of the private foundation tax reform package suitable provisions for correcting abuses that had arisen from the relationships of government officials and private foundations. Even the payment of reasonable and necessary compensation and the reimbursement of reasonable and necessary expenses by a private foundation to a government official are considered as acts of self-dealing under sections 4941(d)(1)(D) and (F) and 4941(d)(2)(E). Furthermore, a private foundation cannot agree to employ a government official unless the agreement to employ him is made within ninety days of his departure from government service. There are certain minor exceptions for transactions with government officials such as the receipt of scholarships and fellowship grants, certain prizes and awards, payments from qualified pension benefit plans, minor non-cash gifts not exceeding $25 a year, and reimbursement or payment for travel expenses solely

---

[27] For purposes of the excess business holdings provision (section 4943), the term "disqualified person" includes a private foundation (1) which is effectively controlled, directly or indirectly, by the same person or persons (other than a bank, trust company, or similar organization acting only as a foundation manager) who control the private foundation in question, or (2) substantially all the contributions to which were made, directly or indirectly, by disqualified persons described in sections 4946(a)(1)(A) through (D) who made, directly or indirectly, substantially all of the contributions to the private foundation in question. The term "controlled" includes any kind of control, direct or indirect, whether legally enforceable and however exercisable and exercised. It is the reality of the control which is decisive—not its form or the mode of exercise. See Reg. section 53.4946-1(b)(1)(i) and Reg. section 1.482-1(a)(3). One or more persons will be considered to have made substantially all of the contributions to a private foundation if such persons have contributed or bequeathed at least 85 percent, and each person has contributed or bequeathed at least 2 percent of the total contributions and bequests (within the meaning of section 507(d)(2) and the regulations thereunder) which have been received by such private foundation during its entire existence; Reg. section 53.4946-1(b)(2).

[28] A "government official" is defined by section 4946(c) to mean an individual who holds any of the following offices at the time of an act of self-dealing: (1) an elective public office in the executive or legislative branch of the United States government; (2) a presidentially appointed office in the executive or judicial branch of the federal government; (3) a position in any branch of the federal government under Civil Service rules, schedule C of rule VI, or which is paid at least as much as the lowest rate of compensation prescribed for GS-16; (4) a position under the U.S. House of Representatives or the Senate at a salary of at least $15,000 per year; (5) an elective or appointive public office in the executive, legislative, or judicial branch of a state or local government, a U.S. possession, or the District of Columbia, at a salary of at least $15,000 per year; or (6) a position as personal or executive assistant or secretary to any of the foregoing.

within the United States not in excess of 125 percent of the maximum government per diem, which is now $25 per day.[29]

As a result of the self-dealing rules, government officials can no longer receive honoraria for their participation in conferences or symposia organized and sponsored by private foundations. It may be asked, however, if there is an inherent abuse either in such participation or in a nominal honorarium so long as a Treasury Department official is not involved. For example, Department of Agriculture and AID officials might be in position to make a meaningful contribution to a symposium sponsored by a private foundation. However, without an honorarium that participation might be lost.

Where disqualified persons engage in acts of self-dealing, two initial taxes are imposed with respect to each act. Although section 4941(a) imposes a tax even though the disqualified person, other than a foundation manager, unknowingly commits an innocent violation of the self-dealing rules, a government official is subject to tax only if he participates in the act *knowing* that it is an act of self-dealing. Moreover, an initial tax is imposed upon any foundation manager who *knowingly* participates in an act of self-dealing, unless such participation is not willful and is due to reasonable cause.[30] Where correction of the act of self-dealing is not made within what is designated as the "correction period," additional taxes are imposed.[31] The maximum amount of initial taxes that can be imposed upon a foundation manager is $10,000; the same limitation is set on additional taxes.[32]

As will be discussed below, sections 4944 and 4945, respectively, also impose taxes on a foundation manager who is a party to an investment that jeopardizes the organization's exempt purpose or agrees to a taxable expenditure if such participation or agreement is *knowing* unless it is not willful and is due to reasonable cause.

The regulations dealing with sections 4941, 4944, and 4945, respectively, define the term "knowing" as used in these provisions. Generally, the term does not mean "having reason to know." Nevertheless, evidence tending to show that a person has reason to know of a particular fact or rule would be relevant in determining whether he had actual knowledge of such fact or rule.

---

[29] See section 4941(d)(2)(G).

[30] Section 4941(a)(2).

[31] Section 4941(b).

[32] Section 4941(c)(2).

56

Specifically, a person is to be considered to have participated in a transaction *knowing* that it is an act of self-dealing, a jeopardizing investment, or a taxable expenditure only if

(1) he had actual knowledge of sufficient facts so that, based solely on such facts, such transaction would be an act of self-dealing, a jeopardizing investment, or a taxable expenditure;

(2) he was aware that such a transaction under these circumstances might violate the provisions of federal tax law governing self-dealing, jeopardizing investments, or taxable expenditures; and

(3) he negligently failed to make reasonable attempts to ascertain whether the transaction was an act of self-dealing, a jeopardizing investment, or a taxable expenditure, or he was in fact aware that it was such an act, investment, or expenditure.[33]

Of all the abuses most frequently raised by foundation critics, self-dealing loomed as one of the most reprehensible. Situations in which donors used their foundations for their personal benefit rather than in the interest of charity were cited by legislators during the hearings in 1969. Section 4941 was a direct response to such abuse. Although the instances of self-dealing may have been few when set against the background of the entire foundation world, it is hard to argue that the absolute prohibition on such acts was not warranted in light of the resulting harm to charity. Moreover, as the Treasury report indicates, an absolute prohibition on certain transactions merely introduces into the tax law a concept which is fundamental to the law of private trusts, that is, "it is better to forbid self-dealing and strike down all such transactions rather than to attempt to separate those transactions which are harmful from those which are not by permitting a fiduciary (as is the donor when he is dealing with charitable funds) to justify his representation of two interests."[34]

One problem raised by section 4941, which might have been handled differently in 1969 and, indeed, might well be the subject of remedial legislation, merits special attention here. Whether for good or evil, many foundations in the past engaged in good faith, fair value business transactions with persons who are now classified as "disqualified." As the result of such transactions (for example, a "bargain sale"), some foundations currently own property which, as a practical matter, cannot be disposed of to anyone except a disqualified person.

---

[33] Regs. sections 53.4941(a)-1(b)(3), 53.4944-1(b)(2)(i), and 53.4945-1(a)(2)(iii).
[34] *Treasury Report*, p. 23.

For example, a private foundation might have a substantial stock interest in a closely held business corporation which is also owned in part by a disqualified person. If the business is not defined as a "business enterprise" within the meaning of section 4943(d)(4) so that the stock interest does not constitute excess business holdings, then the foundation may not be required to dispose of its interest. On the other hand, because the property may not produce current income, it would not be beneficial to the foundation in meeting the minimum payout requirements of section 4942. Nevertheless, the foundation would not be able to dispose of the asset because of the self-dealing rules.

In an effort to alleviate this "lock-in" effect, a special rule might have been included in section 4941(d)(2) which would have provided a grace period for a foundation to dispose of unwanted property at fair market value to a disqualified person without classification of the transaction as an act of self-dealing. Such a rule would not transgress the public interest in light of the announced intention of the Internal Revenue Service to audit all private foundations of any size within the next several years. Any potential harm resulting from disposition at less than fair market value could be corrected on audit, and the goal of the act of benefiting charity would be enhanced by substituting income-producing assets for essentially useless assets.[35]

Minimum Required Distributions—Section 4942

A private foundation, other than an operating foundation,[36] is required to distribute each year an amount equal to the greater of its entire adjusted net income or its minimum investment return, reduced in both cases by the taxes imposed by section 4940 and by subtitle

---

[35] See F. M. Gregory, Jr., "The Congress and Private Foundations—Will the Patient Survive the Operation?" (Speech before the Tax Association's 64th Annual Conference on Taxation, September 27, 1971).

[36] An operating foundation is an organization that makes qualifying distributions directly for the active conduct of the activities constituting the purpose or function for which it is organized and operated equal to substantially all of its adjusted net income and that meets one of the following three requirements:

(1) substantially more than one-half of its assets are devoted directly to such activities;

(2) normally qualifying distributions in an amount not less than two-thirds of its minimum investment return are made directly for the active conduct of such activities;

(3) all its support is normally secured from the general public and from five or more unrelated exempt organizations, not more than 25 percent of such support being received from any one such exempt organization; section 4942(j)(3).

A [37] of the Internal Revenue Code of 1954.[38] This required distribution is referred to as the distributable amount. Once its distributable amount is determined for any given year, the foundation must make qualifying distributions equal to that amount by the end of the following taxable year. Failure to do so creates undistributed income which is subject to tax under section 4942.

The reason that operating foundations are exempt from the statute's minimum distribution requirement under section 4942 is obvious. By definition an operating foundation is required to distribute substantially all of its income in the active conduct of its exempt functions.

Some technical aspects of section 4942 are that a foundation's adjusted net income is defined as the excess of its gross income for the year over the deductions allowed for depletion, depreciation, and for the ordinary and necessary expenses paid or incurred in the production or collection of that gross income. These expenses would include expenses incurred for the management, conservation, or maintenance of property held for the production of gross income.[39] In computing gross income, long-term capital gains are not treated as income for purposes of section 4942 although as noted earlier they are subject to tax under section 4940. Short-term capital gains, however, are treated as income for purposes of section 4942. Additionally, amounts received from the sale of assets, including long-term capital gains, are considered income under section 4942 if the amount paid to acquire the asset in a prior year was treated as a qualifying distribution for such prior year.[40]

The minimum investment return of a private foundation for any given taxable year is a specified percentage of the value of all of its assets other than those that are being used or held for use directly in carrying out its exempt purposes. The specified percentage for foundations organized after May 26, 1969, is 6 percent.[41] For those in existence on that date, only the adjusted net income must be distributed in 1970 and 1971, since the minimum investment return computation does not apply to such institutions until taxable years beginning January 1, 1972. At that time, the specified percentage is phased in starting at 4½ percent and increasing by one-half a per-

---

[37] Subtitle A deals with federal income taxes.
[38] Section 4942(d).
[39] See generally section 4942(f).
[40] Section 4942(f)(2).
[41] Section 4942(e).

centage point until 1975, at which time the 6 percent figure will be applicable.[42]

Since only the excess of the defined distributable amount over qualifying distributions is the undistributed income to which the tax under section 4942 applies, it is important to understand the meaning of the term "qualifying distributions." These are, under section 4942(g)(1), only those amounts, including administrative expenses, paid to accomplish one or more exempt purposes, other than any contribution to (1) an organization controlled, directly or indirectly, by the foundation or one or more disqualified persons,[43] or (2) a nonoperating private foundation. Amounts paid to acquire assets used or held for use in carrying out one or more exempt purposes are also qualifying distributions.[44]

Moreover, amounts which are " set aside"[45] for future payments for exempt purposes are qualifying distributions. For example, a plan to fund a specific research program which is of sufficient magnitude to require an accumulation prior to commencement of the research, even though all the details of the program have not been finalized, constitutes a "set-aside" within the meaning of section 4942(g)(2).

The Internal Revenue Service must be satisfied at the time an amount is "set aside" that such amount is to be paid out for a specific project within five years and that the project can better be accomplished by the accumulation than by the immediate payment of funds.[46]

As indicated earlier, section 4942(g)(1)(A) provides that amounts paid to organizations controlled by the foundation or to nonoperating private foundations are not qualifying distributions. However, section 4942(g)(3) creates a special rule that allows payments to such organizations to constitute qualifying distributions of the donor founda-

---

[42] Section 101(1)(3), Tax Reform Act of 1969. The secretary or his delegate shall determine the applicable percentage for taxable years beginning after 1970. See section 4942(e)(3).

[43] An organization is "controlled" by a foundation or one or more disqualified persons with respect to the foundation if any of such persons may, by aggregating their votes or positions of authority, require the donee organization to make an expenditure, or prevent the donee organization from making an expenditure, regardless of the method by which the control is exercised or exercisable. The "controlled" organization need not be a private foundation. It may be any type of exempt or nonexempt organization. Reg. section 53.4942(a)-3(a)(3).

[44] Section 4942(g)(1)(B).

[45] Section 4942(g)(2).

[46] Ibid. The commissioner's approval must be applied for not later than the end of the taxable year in which the amount is to be set aside. Reg. section 53.4942(a)-3(b)(3).

tion provided such donee organizations expend within the year after the year of receipt a similar amount of their corpus as qualifying distributions and the donor foundation obtains adequate records or other sufficient evidence from the donee organizations showing that such qualifying distributions have been made.[47]

If a foundation has made qualifying distributions for any of its five preceding taxable years which were greater than necessary to avoid tax under section 4942, then the excess may be applied to reduce the amount required to be distributed for a current taxable year.[48]

The regulations issued under section 4942 illustrate the complexities involved in assuring that there is no unreasonable delay in the realization by charity of the benefit flowing from a distribution of a foundation's funds.

One of the more noteworthy provisions in the regulations relates to the treatment of distributions from charitable trusts described in section 4947(a)(1) or (2) for purposes of determining the distributable amount of a foundation for a given year. Treasury Department Regulation section 53.4942(a)-2(b)(1) and (2) make it clear that distributions from wholly charitable trusts described in section 4947(a)(1) shall not increase the distributable amount of a foundation. Moreover, distributions received by a private foundation from a trust created and funded by another person are not to be included in the foundation's gross income for purposes of determining its adjusted net income, except that the income portion of distributions from split-interest trusts described in section 4947(a)(2) with respect to amounts placed in trust after May 26, 1969, is to be added to a foundation's distributable amount.

One question concerning valuation which had been left unanswered by the proposed regulations was how to compute the minimum investment return of a foundation if assets are held by it for only part of a year. Fortunately, this question has been addressed by the final regulations which provide that any asset held for only part of a taxable year shall be taken into account for purposes of determining the foundation's minimum investment return for such year by multiplying the fair market value of such asset by a fraction, the numerator of which is the number of days in such taxable year that the foundation held such asset, and the denominator of which is the number of days in such year.[49]

---

[47] Section 4942(g)(3).

[48] Distributions from pre-1970 years may not be carried over and applied against the section 4942 distribution requirements; section 4942(i).

[49] Reg. section 53.4942(a)-2(c)(4)(vii).

It is also noteworthy that Treasury Department Regulation section 53.4942(a)-3(a)(2)(i) states that reasonable and necessary administrative expenses paid to accomplish one or more exempt purposes described in section 170(c)(2)(B) constitute qualifying distributions. However, under example (1) in those regulations, administrative expenses incurred in earning income would not be qualifying distributions. Therefore, if a foundation's minimum investment return is greater than the adjusted net income, no credit would be allowable for such expenses. However, if the opposite situation should exist (adjusted net income exceeds minimum investment return), the administrative expenses would be deductible from gross income in determining the adjusted net income which must be paid out by the private foundation.

In an effort to avoid unreasonable delay in distributions of funds by private foundations, Congress enacted section 4942. In principle, this objective is justifiable. However, a requirement that a foundation distribute the greater of its net income or 6 percent of its assets could in some cases force a foundation to earn at least 6 percent on its assets in order to maintain merely a constant dollar level in assets.[50]

On the other hand, with a wise investment policy, long-term capital gains can be realized and distributed to meet the payout requirements of section 4942. Nevertheless, section 4942 could cause a dramatic shift in investment practices—a result that is not necessarily consistent with wisdom—or, alternatively, could lead to invasion and erosion of the asset base. To put it another way, foundation managers may well succumb to the temptation to make investments yielding short-term and rapid accumulations of income in lieu of a serious effort to protect and nurture the growth of the underlying assets. On this count, section 4942 tends to move in a direction that opposes the objectives of section 4944, which proscribes investments that jeopardize a foundation's charitable purposes.

Although investments in high-rate bonds or debentures may not constitute jeopardy investments under section 4944, maintenance of a debt security-oriented portfolio would be accompanied by a consequent loss of growth. In short, investment decisions with a view toward short-term results are not necessarily in the best long-range interest of charity.[51]

---

[50] "Private Foundations and the 1969 Tax Reform Act," Columbia Journal of Law and Social Problems, vol. 7 (1971), pp. 240, 273.

[51] Gregory, "Congress and Private Foundations."

Section 4942 may also have an inhibiting effect on the creation of new foundations by donors who desire to contribute stock from their businesses as "seed money" for a personally sponsored charity. Frequently, such stock will not yield as much as the minimum payout requirement. Therefore, rather than risk its sale or distribution by the foundation (where increase in yield would not constitute sound business judgment), these potential donors will simply refrain from creating new charitable foundations.[52]

As indicated earlier, it is hard to quarrel with the purpose and effect of section 4942—dollars will definitely be channeled into the charitable stream. However, the rule itself is harsh in that the rate of payout is high—a fact that had been recognized by the commissioner of internal revenue when he announced that for taxable years beginning in 1972 the applicable percentage for determining the minimum investment return of a private foundation organized after May 26, 1969, was to be reduced from 6 percent to 5½ percent. As to those institutions organized on or before such date, the applicable percentage prescribed by the special rules of section 101(1)(3)(A) of the Tax Reform Act of 1969 was reduced from 4½ percent to 4⅛ percent.[53]

Moreover, the final regulations under section 4942, issued in early February 1973, also recognize this fact, since they provide that the applicable percentage for foundations organized after May 26, 1969, is to be 5½ percent for any calendar year subsequent to 1972, unless a new applicable percentage is published by May 1 of such calendar year.[54]

As for private foundations organized before May 27, 1969, the applicable percentage is to be (1) for taxable years beginning in 1973, the lesser of 5 percent or five-sixths of the applicable percentage prescribed for 1973 for foundations created after May 26, 1969, and (2) for taxable years beginning in 1974, the lesser of 5½ percent or eleven-twelfths of the applicable percentage prescribed for 1974 for foundations organized after May 26, 1969.[55] Thereafter, the applicable percentage is to be the same as that for private foundations organized after May 26, 1969.

---

[52] Ibid.

[53] See Internal Revenue Technical Information Release 1164 (April 17, 1972). Section 4942(e)(3) specifically authorizes the secretary of the treasury or his delegate to change the applicable percentage.

[54] Reg. section 53.4942(a)-2(c)(5)(i)(b).

[55] Reg. section 53.4942(a)-2(c)(5)(ii)(c) and (d).

On April 30, 1973, the Internal Revenue Service announced that the applicable percentages to be used for taxable years beginning in 1973 is 5.25 percent in the case of foundations organized after May 26, 1969, and 4.375 percent (five-sixths of 5.25 percent) in the case of foundations organized before May 27, 1969.[56]

In January 1972, the Ways and Means Committee of the House of Representatives acknowledged the problems inherent in the application of section 4942 in reporting a bill which would have reduced the minimum payout to 5 percent and would have permitted foundations until 1978 to reach that distribution level.[57] The required payout would have started at 3½ percent for 1972 and would have been increased by half a percentage point every two years. The reasons for this bill, as stated by that committee, were that the higher rate of 6 percent

> may well have damaging effects on the continued viability of many foundations. Additionally the phase-in period provided for foundations organized before May 27, 1969, will not afford sufficient time to properly rearrange their investment and payout patterns so as to efficiently comply with the law's charitable distribution requirements.

The logic is sound and the need is certainly present, but the bill died with the adjournment of Congress in December 1972.

Tax on Excess Business Holdings—Section 4943

A private foundation is not prohibited from owning an interest in a business enterprise; rather, its holdings are limited by section 4943 to a specified percentage of the total holdings in a particular business. Regulations under section 4943 were first proposed and published on January 3, 1973. Although these regulations, in general, do offer a reasonable and practical interpretation of admittedly complex statutory provisions, they also appear in some respects to compound the complexities and intricacies of the statute. Moreover, these regulations do not in all regards appear premised upon a literal construction of the statute, and thus are evidently a reflection of policy positions of the Internal Revenue Service and of the Treasury.

Turning now to a discussion of some of the general rules of the statute and the proposed regulations, in the case of a corporation a private foundation may own stock representing as much as 20 percent

---

[56] Technical Information Release 1242, April 30, 1973.
[57] House Report No. 92-791, 92d Congress, 2d session (1972), accompanying H.R. 11197.

of the voting power of such corporation, reduced, however, by stock representing the percentage of the voting power owned by all disqualified persons. In other words, the amount of stock representing voting power held by disqualified persons in a particular corporation proportionately reduces the amount of such stock representing voting power which may be held by a private foundation.

In the event that a private foundation has holdings in excess of the amount permitted by the statute, known as "permitted holdings," section 4943(a)(1) imposes a tax equal to 5 percent of the value of the business holdings in excess of the permitted holdings. Additional taxes are imposed if the foundation still has excess business holdings after a specified period of time.

Specifically, the term "excess business holdings"[58] is defined as the amount of stock or other interest in a business enterprise[59] which the foundation would have to dispose of, to other than disqualified persons, in order for the remainder to constitute permitted holdings.[60] As indicated earlier, a foundation's permitted holdings are generally limited to stock representing 20 percent of the voting power reduced by stock representing the percentage of voting power held by all disqualified persons.[61]

Where it is established that effective control of a corporation is held by one or more persons who are not disqualified persons, the 20 percent limitation is raised to 35 percent by section 4943(c)(2)(B). Furthermore, a *de minimis* rule applies where a foundation owns not more than 2 percent of the voting power and not more than 2 percent of the value of all outstanding shares of all classes of stock.[62] In that

---

[58] Section 4943(c)(1). Business holdings are not limited to stock ownership in corporate enterprises, but include holdings in unincorporated enterprises, such as partnerships; see section 4943(c)(3). Permitted holdings in such noncorporate enterprises are to be determined under regulations prescribed by the Treasury. There are to be no permitted holdings in sole proprietorships.

[59] For purposes of section 4943, a business enterprise does not include a functionally related business nor a trade or business in which at least 95 percent of the gross income is from passive sources; section 4943(d)(4).

[60] Section 4943(c)(1).

[61] Section 4943(c)(2)(A). Nonvoting stock may be held without limitation only if disqualified persons own stock representing 20 percent or less of the voting power.

[62] For purposes of section 4943, the term "disqualified person" includes other foundations that are either effectively controlled by the same persons who control the particular foundation, or have received substantially all of their contributions from persons who are disqualified with respect to that foundation; see section 4946(a)(1)(H). In computing the 2 percent *de minimis* rule, the excess business holdings of other private foundations described in section 4946(a)(1)(H) are to be aggregated with that of the foundation attempting to meet the *de minimis* rule.

event, the foundation is not treated as having excess business holdings in that corporation irrespective of the holdings of disqualified persons.[63]

Where excess business holdings are acquired by a foundation after May 26, 1969, other than by purchase (for example, by gift or bequest), the foundation has in effect a five-year divestiture period in which to dispose of its excess holdings without incurring the tax imposed by section 4943.

If a foundation has excess business holdings on May 26, 1969, all interests which such foundation holds, actually or constructively, in the enterprise on such date shall, while held by the foundation, be deemed held by a disqualified person during a period of time known as the first phase. Thus, such a foundation cannot have excess business holdings with respect to such business interests during the first phase.

The first phase may be one of several different time periods, depending upon the holdings of the foundation, or of the foundation and all disqualified persons, on May 26, 1969.

If the foundation itself owned more than 95 percent of the voting stock, the first phase consists of a twenty-year period. If the foundation and all disqualified persons together had more than a 75 percent voting interest or owned more than 75 percent of the value of all outstanding shares of all classes of stock, or comparable interests in an unincorporated enterprise, the first phase is a fifteen-year period. In all other cases, the first phase consists of a ten-year period.

At the end of the first phase, the combined holdings of the disqualified persons and the foundation must be reduced so that they do not exceed either 50 percent of the voting power or 50 percent of the value of all outstanding shares of all other classes of stock. Thereafter, the second phase begins. If, at any time during the second phase, disqualified persons own more than 2 percent of the voting power, the foundation's holdings may not exceed 25 percent of the voting power or 25 percent of the value of all outstanding shares of all classes of stock.

According to Proposed Regulation section 53.4943-4(c)(2)(ii), the 25 percent limitation is to apply for the time remaining in the second phase after the first day during the second phase on which such disqualified persons together hold more than 2 percent of the voting power.

The third phase means all periods following the second phase. If, immediately before the close of the second phase, the 25 percent

---

[63] Section 4943(c)(2)(C).

limitation described above did not apply, then the total holdings of the foundation during the third phase may not exceed 35 percent of the voting power reduced by the voting power held by disqualified persons, or 35 percent of the value of all outstanding shares of all classes of stock reduced by the percentage of value of all outstanding shares of all classes of stock held by disqualified persons. If the 35 percent limitation applies, then the foundation's holdings may not exceed 25 percent of the voting power or 25 percent of the value of all outstanding shares of all classes of stock if, at any time during the third phase, all disqualified persons together hold more than 2 percent of the voting power. The limitations of the preceding sentence shall apply for the period occurring after that day during the third phase in which such disqualified persons hold more than 2 percent of the voting power.[64]

The "present holdings" rules described above are designed to provide private foundations which had excess business holdings on May 26, 1969, prior to the passage of the Tax Reform Act, adequate time for orderly compliance with the divestiture rules. Accordingly, the divestiture periods are geared to the amount of holdings—the greater the holdings on May 26, 1969, the more time permitted for divestiture.

According to the Peterson Commission, the history of foundations, and in particular that of the larger foundations, indicates that they were frequently created through contributions of stock—usually blocks of stock controlling a business which the donor had developed during his lifetime. The data compiled by the Peterson Commission reveals that over two-fifths of all gifts to foundations were in the form of control stock. Section 4943 is directed precisely at discouraging the contribution of this type of asset. No comparable provision appeared in prior law. However, as indicated earlier in the discussion of the House proposals in 1950, the House of Representatives did propose to disallow the charitable contribution deduction if the contribution consisted of stock in a closely held company and if the contribution was to a controlled foundation.[65]

The following arguments were advanced in 1969 in support of the excess business holdings provisions and, if they seem familiar, it is because most of them were contained in the Treasury report in 1965:

(1) Where private foundations own substantial amounts of stock in corporations, there is a tendency to use the foun-

---

[64] Proposed Regulation section 53.4943-4(d)(2)(ii).
[65] See note 19, Chapter 3.

dation's stockholdings to assert business control and to ignore the production of income by the foundation to be used for charitable purposes. The interests of the foundation's managers are diverted to the maintenance and improvement of the business and away from their charitable duties.

(2) Even where the ownership of a business by a private foundation does not cause the foundation managers to neglect their charitable duties, the corporate business may be run in such a way that it unfairly competes with other businesses whose owners must pay taxes on the income they realize.

(3) The divestiture requirements are sufficiently gradual (especially in the case of existing holdings) so as not to unreasonably disrupt the foundation's investment plans and also the worth of the security being divested. Even as to the future, 5 years should be sufficient where the excess holdings develop after knowledge of the new rules.

(4) Requiring divestiture is better than denying deductions because it permits a donor to give valuable assets to a foundation while allowing the foundation sufficient time to make the assets useful to it.[66]

Let us consider each of the foregoing arguments. First, in light of the payout requirements of section 4942, foundation managers will be unable to ignore their responsibility to produce and use income for charitable purposes because failure to do so will eventually precipitate the sale or distribution of the foundation's assets (that is, control stock).

As to the statement that foundation managers are diverted from their duties to charity in an effort to maintain and improve business, it is interesting to note that there are only approximately 1,200 to 1,500 full-time professionals managing foundations and about 400 of these are associated with the Ford and Rockefeller foundations.[67] These figures suggest that, independent of the question of whether or not a foundation has excess business holdings, there are just not enough full-time professional foundation managers willing to devote their total efforts to a foundation's charitable purposes. Most foun-

---

[66] See summary of H.R. 13270, The Tax Reform Act of 1969 (as passed by the House of Representatives), prepared by the staffs of the Joint Committee on Internal Revenue Taxation and the Committee on Finance, p. 15.

[67] H. Dressner, panel discussion on "Assessment of Present and Anticipated Capacity of Private Foundations to Fulfill Expected Philanthropic Functions in Light of 1969 Legislation," *Tax Institute of America Symposium on Impact of Taxes on Philanthropy*, December 2, 1971.

dation managers serve for little pay and thus devote only part of their time to foundation matters and therefore their situation is comparable to foundations whose managers spend substantial time on business interests. This similarity suggests that the interest of a foundation manager in business offers no justification for stripping the foundation of its business holdings. Moreover, a manager who spends substantial time and energy on a foundation's business interests would not necessarily be engaged in activity detrimental to charity, especially since section 4942 will insure current distributions to charity.[68]

The second argument advanced by advocates of section 4943 was also raised during legislative debate preceding the passage of the Revenue Act of 1950 and resulted in the enactment of the tax on unrelated business income and the feeder organization rule.[69] Adequate enforcement of these provisions would help considerably to remove this objection. Furthermore, even assuming that a donor's business may benefit from foundation control of his business, the donor has made an irrevocable commitment to charity, and section 4942 will guarantee that the stock of the donor's business will produce a fair return to charity.

The third argument is not so much a justification for the excess business holdings provision as much as it is a palliative measure to delay its effect in the event of failure to comply.

As to the last argument, it also is more in the nature of a sweetening of the medicine once it has been prescribed, but it hardly approaches a justification for section 4943.

Obviously, inherent in the rationale underlying section 4943 is the belief that there is something fundamentally objectionable and incompatible with a foundation's effort to serve both charity and the business interests of the donor. As one commentator has stated, the reasons for the approach of section 4943

> were not so much regulatory as theological. It derives from the Sermon on the Mount, in which we are told that "ye cannot serve both God and mammon." It is ironic that under the Tax Reform Act an organization *can* serve both God and mammon by holding corporate control stock if it is a church, a school, or some other non-foundation charity. In the excess business holdings area . . . Congress singled out only the private foundations. As a result, the abuses that can exist when a donor uses charity as a way of maintaining

---

[68] See Gregory, "Congress and Private Foundations."
[69] See discussion, p. 20.

control of his business enterprise may well continue. There are hundreds or thousands of financially hard-pressed colleges and churches which would be delighted to receive control stock, with all kinds of informal voting understandings. And for such a church or such a school there are no self-dealing rules. . . . Thus, to the extent that corporate control stock now is diverted from foundations to non-foundation charities, we may be worse off from a regulatory viewpoint.[70]

One can only speculate about the inhibiting effect of section 4943 on the creation of new foundations. Along that line, the Peterson Commission expressed its concern in the following terms:

Other provisions in the new law may also discourage the establishment of new foundations. . . .

We also objected to the way the new law limits foundation ownership of corporate control stock. One of the major and understandable concerns about foundation holdings of such blocks of stock has been that they may be given to foundations for reasons such as protecting the donor's control of the corporation, which have nothing to do with their desirability from an investment standpoint and the best long-term interests of charity. In our view, this concern is substantially reduced when such holdings must make a significant, annual contribution to charity. A high payout requirement, prohibitions on self-dealing, and greater disclosure—all required by the new law—seem to us to provide a better solution than an arbitrary limit on percentage of ownership, especially if coupled with greatly improved government supervision of foundations. We believe that this provision could easily retard the flow of large pools of capital into philanthropy.[71]

Investments Jeopardizing Charitable Purposes—Section 4944

Section 4944 imposes a tax on a foundation and its manager where, on or after January 1, 1970, an investment of income or corpus is made which jeopardizes the carrying out of the foundation's exempt purposes.[72] However, an important exception is specifically provided by statute. Under section 4944(c) "program related investments" are not to be considered as jeopardizing investments where their primary purpose is to accomplish one or more of the objectives described in

---

[70] J. G. Simon, "Some Under-Publicized Consequences," in *Tax Problems of Non-Profit Organizations*, pp. 195, 199.

[71] *Peterson Commission Report*, pp. 166-167.

[72] This provision replaces section 504(a)(3) of the 1954 code before amendment in 1969.

section 170(c)(2)(B) (for example, religious, charitable, and educational purposes) and where no significant purpose of the investment is the production of income or the appreciation of property.

The determination of whether investments jeopardize the carrying out of a foundation's charitable purposes is to be made as of the time of the investment in accordance with a "prudent trustee" approach, and not subsequently on the basis of hindsight after a loss occurs.[73]

Similar to section 4941(a)(2) is section 4944(a)(2) which deals with a seeming contradiction in terms in that it imposes an initial excise tax on a foundation manager who makes an investment "knowing" that it is a jeopardizing investment, but forgives the act (and the tax) if the investment is not "willful" and is due to reasonable cause.[74]

This study has already dealt with the definition of the term "knowing" as used in sections 4941, 4944, and 4945. Participation by a foundation manager is considered "willful" if it is voluntary, conscious, and intentional, but it cannot be willful if he does not know he is participating in self-dealing or in making a jeopardizing investment or that he is agreeing to a taxable expenditure.[75]

Interestingly, the regulations under these three provisions (sections 4941, 4944, 4945) state that a person's participation in an act of self-dealing or in making a jeopardy investment or in agreeing to make a taxable expenditure will ordinarily not be considered "knowing" or "willful" and will ordinarily be considered "due to reasonable cause" if, after full disclosure of the factual situation to legal counsel, he relies on the advice of such counsel expressed in a reasoned written legal opinion that an act is not an act of self-dealing, an investment is not a jeopardizing investment, or an expenditure is not a taxable expenditure.[76]

Section 4944 was designed to prevent imprudent investments by foundations. However, this provision is not new and was enacted to preserve the rule of section 504(a)(3) which was repealed by the Tax Reform Act. As indicated earlier, the determination under section 4944 as to whether a particular investment carries out a

---

[73] See Joint Committee on Internal Revenue Taxation, *General Explanation of the Tax Reform Act*, p. 46, and Reg. section 53.4944-1(a)(2)(i).

[74] Section 4945(a)(2) also imposes a tax on a foundation manager who agrees to make a taxable expenditure *knowing* it to be such, unless his agreement is not willful and due to reasonable cause.

[75] Regs. sections 53.4941(a)-1(b)(4), 53.4944-1(b)(2)(ii) and 53.4945-1(a)(2)(iv).

[76] Regs. sections 53.4941(a)-(b)(6), 53.4944-1(b)(2)(v) and 53.4945-1(a)(2)(vi).

foundation's charitable purposes is to be made at the time of the investment in accordance with a "prudent trustee" approach, and not subsequently on the basis of hindsight after a loss occurs. Therefore, great weight should be accorded to the informed judgment of foundation managers on the investments they make. The regulations under section 4944 encourage this philosophy. The enforcement and audit program of the Internal Revenue Service will, it is hoped, do no less.[77]

In short, section 4944 should not be viewed as an invitation to revenue agents to assume the role of investment advisor. Furthermore, too rigid enforcement of section 4944 could stimulate conservative investment policies. Investment in "blue chip" stocks might satisfy the proscription of this section but it could entail gradual, continuous distribution of the foundation's assets if a manager is not to run afoul of section 4942. Therefore, Internal Revenue Service audit policies may well be the decisive factor under this provision.

Taxable Expenditures—Section 4945

The fifth and last excise tax is imposed on private foundations by section 4945[78] and relates to any "taxable expenditure." This term is defined to mean any amount paid or cost incurred by a private foundation

(1) to carry on propaganda, or otherwise attempt to influence legislation;[79]

(2) to influence the outcome of any specific public election,

---

[77] An overzealous enforcement program could create the anomalous result of an investment which does not jeopardize the carrying out of a foundation's exempt purposes but which yields too low an income return to satisfy the section 4942 distribution requirements.

[78] Of all the private foundation provisions, section 4945 was perhaps the least expected.

[79] Section 4945(e) defines the type of legislative activity that meets the definition of a taxable expenditure as: (1) any attempt to influence any legislation through attempts to affect the opinion of the general public or any segment thereof; and (2) any attempt to influence legislation through communications with any member or employee of a legislative body, or with any other government official or employee who may participate in the formulation of the legislation (except technical advice or assistance provided to a government body or to a committee or other subdivision, as the case may be). The legislative activity prohibition does not preclude nonpartisan analysis, study, or research. Furthermore, section 4945(e)(2) does not apply to any amount paid or incurred in connection with an appearance before, or communication to, any legislative body with respect to a possible decision of such body which might affect the existence of the private foundation, its powers and duties, its tax-exempt status, or the deduction of contributions thereto.

or to carry on, directly or indirectly, any voter registration drive, unless certain conditions are met; [80]

(3) as a grant to an individual for travel, study, or other similar purposes, unless the grant satisfies certain requirements;

(4) as a grant to an organization which is not a public charity, unless the foundation exercises expenditure responsibility; and

(5) for any purpose other than an exempt purpose described in section 170(c)(2)(B).

Section 501(c)(3) provides exemption only if no substantial part of the activities of an organization is carrying on propaganda or otherwise attempting to influence legislation. Section 4945(d)(1) and (e) in effect removes the "substantiality" test contained in section 501(c)(3) in determining whether a private foundation has made a taxable expenditure.[81]

As for grants to individuals, section 4945(g) provides that such grants are not proscribed if awarded on an objective and nondiscriminating basis and if the grant

(1) constitutes a scholarship or fellowship grant which is excludible from the grantee's income under section 117(a) [82]

---

[80] In connection with amounts paid to influence the outcome of specific public elections or to carry on voter registration drives, section 4945(f) provides that the proscription against those activities will not apply to any amount paid or incurred by any section 501(c)(3) organization:

(1) the activities of which are nonpartisan, are carried on in five or more states, and are not confined to one specific election;

(2) substantially all the income of which is expended directly for the active conduct of its exempt purposes;

(3) substantially all the support, not including gross investment income, of which is received, over a five-year period from (a) exempt organizations, the general public, or governmental units with no one exempt organization contributing more than 25 percent of such support, and (b) not more than half of its support from gross investment income; and

(4) which does not receive contributions that are specifically restricted for use in certain states, political subdivisions, the District of Columbia, or in certain election periods.

[81] See Joint Committee on Internal Revenue Taxation, *General Explanation of the Tax Reform Act*, p. 83.

[82] Section 117(a) provides that, in the case of an individual, gross income does not include

(1) any amount received—
  (A) as a scholarship at an educational institution, or
  (B) as a fellowship grant, including the value of contributed services and accommodation, and

(2) any amount received to cover expenses for travel, research, clerical help, or equipment which are incidental to such a scholarship or to a fellowship grant but only to the extent that the amount is so expended by the recipient.

and is used for study at educational institutions;[83]

(2) constitutes a prize or award, if the recipient is selected from the general public, which is excludible from the recipient's gross income under section 74(b);[84] or

(3) has as its purpose to achieve a specific objective, produce a report or similar product, or improve or enhance a literary, artistic, scientific, or similar skill or talent of the grantee.

Grants to other private foundations can be made only if the granting foundation assumes expenditure responsibility, which means that it must exert all reasonable efforts and establish adequate procedures to insure that the grant is expended solely for the purpose for which made, to obtain complete reports from the grantee on how the funds are spent, and to prepare and submit complete and detailed reports to the Internal Revenue Service on such expenditures.[85]

For purposes of section 4945, the term "grants" to individuals and organizations other than public charities includes, but is not limited to, scholarships, fellowships, internships, prizes, awards, as well as loans for charitable purposes described in section 170(c)(2)(B) and "program-related investments," as defined in section 4944. Moreover, "grants" include payments to exempt organizations for their exempt purposes whether or not such payments are solicited by the recipient organizations.[86]

Expenditures to acquire investments to produce income for exempt purposes, to pay taxes, and to cover the reasonable expenses of investments are all excepted from the term "taxable expenditures," as are any payments that constitute qualifying distributions under section 4942(g) or allowable deductions under section 4940. However, expenditures for unreasonable administrative expenses, including compensation, consultant fees and other fees for services rendered such as attorneys' fees, will ordinarily be taxable expenditures unless

---

[83] "Educational institution" as used here refers to one that normally maintains a regular faculty and curriculum and normally has a regular organized body of students in attendance; see section 151(e)(4).

[84] Section 74(b) provides that gross income does not include amounts received as prizes and awards made primarily in recognition of religious, charitable, scientific, educational, artistic, literary, or civic achievements, but only if

(1) the recipient was selected without any action on his part to enter the contest or proceeding; and

(2) the recipient is not required to render substantial future services as a condition to receiving the prize or award.

[85] See section 4945(h).

[86] Reg. sections 53.4945-4(a)(2) and 43.4945-5(a)(2).

the foundation is able to demonstrate that such expenses were paid or incurred in the good faith belief that they were reasonable and that ordinary business care and prudence were exercised in the payment or incurrence of such expenses in such amounts.[87]

If a foundation distributes its funds to hospitals, schools, or churches, it is unlikely that such distribution constitutes a taxable expenditure under section 4945, especially if it is in the nature of a general support grant to such institutions. As a consequence, many foundations may well try to "play it safe" and make grants only for traditional section 501(c)(3) purposes. Herein lies the principal objection to section 4945—that is, foundation managers may become cautious, with the result that innovative and even the controversial projects will be the loser. "The role of foundations . . . is to direct their funds, in substantial measure at least, to new and innovative programs not subject to a wide or popular base of philanthropic support."[88]

The regulations under section 4945 have generally adopted a reasonable approach to its interpretation. The approach of the Internal Revenue Service in its audit program will apparently also be reasonable, as is reflected in the remarks of K. Martin Worthy, former chief counsel of the Internal Revenue Service, in his address to the Southwestern Legal Foundation. Mr. Worthy stated it would be most unfortunate for the foundations to continue to operate with only the government providing the "rules of the road." Moreover, he commented that the Internal Revenue Service is committed to making the tax system as responsive as possible to changing concepts of charity.

Certainly section 4945 will necessitate thorough investigation, detailed information, and thus extensive record-keeping in connection with the making of grants.

> When this fact is added to whatever degree of natural caution and conservativeness a foundation already has and is added to its awareness of the climate of public and Congressional disapprobation—even hostility—in which it feels it operates, a strong incentive can build up to avoid controversial grants altogether. This human tendency may in fact be more indicative of the real danger of the new law than is any specific provision of it.[89]

---

[87] Reg. section 53.4945-6(b).

[88] Creel, "Problems Posed for Larger Foundations," p. 186.

[89] *New York Times,* June 1, 1970, p. 29, as quoted in "Private Foundations and the 1969 Tax Reform Act," p. 271.

Other commentators have expressed similar views on the effect of section 4945 on the vitality of foundations in our democratic society.

> Whether or not excessive regulation limits power, it has the effect (both in industry and in philanthropy) of *impairing innovation*. When an administrator is preoccupied with legal thickets and afraid of penalties and courts (and, in the case of smaller foundations, afraid of the legal costs of getting into trouble), one natural reaction is to stay on main roads, well-traveled, known to be trouble free. . . . [F]ear of making a mistake . . . will discourage grants to some of the less orthodox groups or individuals.[90] [Emphasis added.]

The answer to these comments is for the foundations to act fearlessly, responsibly, and innovatively. But the smaller foundations, at least, are not prepared to lay their heads on the chopping block, even though the block will not in all likelihood become bloodied. For example, one foundation with assets of over $10 million has not been making any grants because it is too concerned over the effects which the Tax Reform Act and an Internal Revenue Service audit might have on its operations. Such a reaction is understandable, but if a foundation with over $10 million in assets demonstrates such paralysis in the face of the new provisions, then the foundation world faces some unneeded fundamental change.

Administrative Problems and Costs

The foregoing discussion concentrates on the five substantive rules applicable to private foundations.[91] In addition to those rules, there are a number of procedural requirements imposed on private foundations.

Section 508(e)(1) requires each private foundation to incorporate in its government instrument provisions which will require it to make

---

[90] Simon, "Some Under-Publicized Consequences," p. 202.

[91] In an effort to eliminate the potential for avoiding the private foundation rules through the use of nonexempt charitable trusts, Congress enacted section 4947, the essence of which is generally to subject such trusts to most of the same restrictions and requirements that are imposed on private foundations. The applicable restrictions are those relating to termination of private foundation status (section 507), governing instruments (section 508(e)), self-dealing, retention of excess business holdings, and the making of speculative investments and taxable expenditures. Additionally, the current income payout requirement and the 4 percent excise tax on net investment income are made applicable, but only where all the interests in the trusts are devoted to section 170(c)(2)(B) purposes.

timely distributions of income,[92] and which will prohibit self-dealing,[93] retention of excess business holdings,[94] speculative investments,[95] and taxable expenditures.[96]

In recognition of the fact that section 508(e) could be a trap for the unwary private foundations and charitable trusts in existence on December 31, 1969, the regulations issued under section 508(e) provide that governing instruments shall be deemed to have been amended to comply with section 508(e) if valid provisions of state law are enacted which require the private foundation to act in accordance with sections 4941 through 4945 or which treat the required provisions as if they are contained in the foundation's governing instrument.[97] Moreover, the regulations create a transitional rule whereby, in connection with tax deductions for gifts or bequests made before a specified date, section 508(e)(1) shall not apply to any foundation, regardless of when organized, with respect to

(1) any taxable year beginning before the transitional date;

(2) any period on or after the transitional date during the pendency of any judicial proceeding commenced before the transitional date by the foundation which is necessary to reform or excuse it from compliance with its governing instrument or any other instrument in order to meet the requirements of section 508(e)(1); and

(3) any period after the termination of any such judicial proceeding during which its governing instrument or any other instrument does not permit it to meet the requirements of section 508(e)(1).

For these purposes, the transitional date means the earlier of either the ninety-first day after regulations under section 170(b)(1)(A) become final or the ninety-first day after the date an organization receives a final ruling or determination that it is a private foundation under section 509(a).[98]

Failure to comply with section 508(e) will result in loss of exemption under section 501(a) and in loss of eligibility as a charitable organization to which contributions are deductible.

The Tax Reform Act of 1969 also imposed new reporting requirements on private foundations.[99] Every private foundation must

---

92 Section 4942.
93 Section 4941.
94 Section 4943.
95 Section 4944.
96 Section 4945.
97 Reg. section 1.508-3(g).
98 Ibid.
99 Under prior law, exempt organizations, other than religious organizations and certain of their affiliates, schools and colleges, publicly supported charitable

file two separate annual returns—an information return and a report.[100] The Form 990 annual information return must contain the following: gross income, expenses, assets and liabilities, disbursements for exempt purposes, contributions and gifts received, names and addresses of all substantial contributors, names and addresses of managers and highly compensated employees, and the compensation paid to them.[101] Failure to file the information return results in a sanction on the organization of $10 per day up to a $5,000 maximum on any one return, unless reasonable cause is shown.[102]

In addition to the information return, section 6056 requires every private foundation with assets of $5,000 or more to file an annual report for taxable years beginning after December 31, 1969.[103] This report must be made available for public inspection. A notice indicating that it is available must be published not later than the date prescribed for filing the report in a newspaper of general circulation in the county in which the principal office of the foundation is located.[104]

The regulations under section 6056 also provide that copies of the annual report are to be sent by foundation managers to the attorney general of each state having jurisdiction with respect to a private foundation, its assets, or its activities. Furthermore, any state requesting the report is entitled to receive it.[105] Appropriate state

organizations, certain fraternal beneficiary societies, and federally owned congressionally chartered exempt organizations, were required to file annual information returns indicating gross income, expenses, disbursements for exempt purposes, accumulations, balance sheets, and the total amount of contributions and gifts received during the year. Failure to file such returns did not incur any specific sanctions, other than criminal sanctions in extreme cases. The information required to be provided was open to the public.

[100] The Form 990 annual information return must be filed by every exempt organization except churches and their auxiliary organizations, any organization which is not a private foundation and which has gross receipts of $5,000 or less in each taxable year, and the exclusively religious activities of any religious order; see section 6033(a)(2).

[101] Reg. section 1.6033-2(a)(2)(ii).

[102] Section 6652(d)(1).

[103] Section 6056. The information required on the annual report includes the total contributions and gifts received, itemized list of all grants and contributions that have been made or approved for future payment, names and addresses of recipients, relationship, if any, between recipients and foundation managers or substantial contributors, a concise statement of the purpose of each grant or contribution, addresses of all foundation managers who are substantial contributors or who own 10 percent or more of any organization of which the foundation owns 10 percent or more, and address of the principal office of the foundation.

[104] Section 6104(d).

[105] Reg. section 1.6056-1(b)(3).

officials will also be notified as to certain events concerning private foundations, such as a final determination by the Internal Revenue Service that an organization is no longer exempt from tax under section 501(c)(3) or that a tax has been imposed on a private foundation as a result of a violation of one of the rules in chapter 42 of the Internal Revenue Code.[106]

As is evident, the new private foundation rules impose new demands and burdens on the staffs of foundations. Bearing in mind that very few are professionally staffed, the burdens become even more onerous.

Other requirements in this category bear some examination. For example, a private foundation must identify those individuals and organizations which are classified as "disqualified persons." This cannot and should not be a random or careless exercise because if the foundation, substantial contributors, and foundation managers are to avoid severe penalties, accurate identification is important in order to avoid violation of the provisions on self-dealing.

In addition, the business interests of this group of "disqualified persons," including certain related private foundations, are to be aggregated in order to determine whether a private foundation has excess business holdings subject to tax under section 4943. To make matters more interesting, these determinations must be made continuously so that the foundation can be sure that excess business holdings are not created inadvertently in the future through a stock purchase by a "disqualified person."

A foundation which makes grants to individuals must secure an advance ruling from the Internal Revenue Service approving the procedures and rules under which such grants are made. In order to obtain a favorable ruling, regulations require the foundation to take an impressive series of steps to create a class of candidates from which grantees might be selected and to devise follow-up procedures to be invoked following the award of the grant. These include reports reflecting the grantee's progress in achieving the purpose of the grant.

If the foundation makes grants to organizations which by definition are not excluded from the status of private foundation under section 509(a)(1), (2), or (3), "expenditure responsibility" must be exercised. This, as indicated earlier, carries with it a number of

---

[106] Reg. section 301.6104-3(a). A return on Form 4720 which gives details as to any transaction which may result in the imposition of a tax under chapter 42 must be filed with the Internal Revenue Service and must identify the alleged transaction as nontaxable.

obligations that the private foundation must discharge. It must (a) make a pre-grant inquiry concerning the potential grantee which is complete enough to assure a reasonable man that the grantee will use the grant for the proper purposes; (b) secure a written agreement from the grantee that the funds will be used only for the purposes specified in the grant letter; (c) secure detailed reports from the grantee that will establish that the purposes and objectives of the grant are being met; and (d) in addition to other follow-up procedures, make full and complete reports to the Internal Revenue Service with respect to such grants.

The genesis of the underlying rationale of these provisions is quite apparent. However, so much administrative detail seems inordinately comprehensive and burdensome for the admittedly legitimate purpose to be achieved. If each of these requirements is evaluated in isolation, it is difficult for the most part to quarrel with it. But, the cumulative effect of all of them is substantial and experience may well show that they should be re-evaluated. The test should be whether the cost and the burdens are justified by the results achieved; or whether the end sought can be realized with a set of fewer and less burdensome requirements.

In the interim there will be pain and suffering that will vary depending upon the size of the foundation. In the case of the large foundations these new administrative requirements will, at the least, be troublesome. However, additions to their professional staff should enable these institutions to cope with the problem.

However, there are many small foundations without professional staffs and whose resources should be husbanded for charitable purposes. Some advocate that such private foundations should simply terminate their status and give all their assets to one or more public charities; the idea would be that the public charity would administer the small foundation's program. Others have suggested that such foundations terminate their status and give all their assets to community foundations. Either course may in fact be required, given the new administrative burden placed on the foundations.

It is entirely possible that, with experience, these burdens will not prove so great. These very viable institutions may learn to adapt very well to the new requirements. On the other hand, the latter are not carved in stone, and if they represent considerably more than what is necessary to achieve the intent of the statute, some modification seems clearly in order—particularly if matters of administration are not to take on a too dominant role with respect to the creation or continued life of a private foundation.

Obviously, the administrative tasks will increase administrative costs. One commentator estimated that the additional expense would add a good 10 percent, or perhaps 15 percent, to administrative costs, at least during the first years after passage of the Tax Reform Act.[107] These expenses, of course, also reduce the amount available for charitable purposes.

Smaller foundations will feel the effects of increased administrative costs to a much greater extent than the larger foundations which can afford to maintain their own legal staffs. Thus, these smaller foundations may lose their efficacy and vitality in the area of innovative charitable work. It is anomalous that smaller foundations may be prevented from hiring additional staff because the cost of maintaining that staff may be unreasonable in relation to its net income.

The administrative tasks and expenses confronting private foundations under the Tax Reform Act have led one commentator to conclude that the act may aggravate monopoly or oligopoly in the foundation world. In his words:

> It may seem strange to talk of monopoly or oligopoly in a world populated by some 24,000 charitable foundations. Yet only three hundred of these foundations, approximately, have assets in excess of ten million dollars and therefore have a substantial and continuing capacity to help finance new ventures. Moreover, in any one area of the country or in any one field of work, only a few of these three hundred foundations are likely to be available to help those who need such start-up assistance. And within this group of three hundred, some foundations may dissolve over time, and some will develop very tired blood.
>
> There is a baleful effect on a foundation which arises from its status as the only substantial foundation (or one of the few substantial foundations) that resides in a particular state or region or that deals with a particular topic—to be the only foundation interested in urban design in New England, for example, or the only foundation in the Southwest interested in mental health. If this foundation says "no" to an applicant, that answer may represent the applicant's first, second, and third strikes. A foundation in this situation may find itself developing a sense of responsibility for all comers, with the result that it may try to provide some small, fractional solace to all who knock on its door. This is not the way to promote adventurous philanthropy.
>
> Viewed from the outside, the problem is even worse, for as a matter of public policy—in terms of increasing the capacity

---

[107] Creel, "Problems Posed for Larger Foundations," p. 186.

of our society to respond to its vast challenges and crises—there is a need to offer a variety of funding options to those who have new ideas for solving our problems.

Accordingly, here in the field of private *charitable* enterprise, as in the area of private *commercial* enterprise, we need a reasonable rate of new entry—in other words, a reasonable birth rate for new foundations. Such a birth rate is discouraged under the Tax Reform Act. It is discouraged partly because of the complexity of the regulatory system, and partly because of the fifty-percent, twenty-percent contribution ceiling differential, which discriminates against the foundations. But the birth rate is mainly discouraged by two other provisions: the provision dealing with the deductibility of gifts of appreciated property, and the provision dealing with excess business holdings.[108]

In addition to the decreasing birth rate of new foundations, the Tax Reform Act has precipitated situations in which small foundations have decided to terminate their status in the face of complicated and massive legislation and "leave the job to the big boys." [109] The decreasing birth rate and the increasing death rate among small private foundations will have a detrimental effect on the pluralism of our social order. Individuals may decide that it is no longer worthwhile to seek to express their own bents, concerns, and experience by establishing and maintaining foundations dedicated to new charitable endeavors. If they do, our society will be the loser.

Other individuals, who have served society well by devoting their time and talents to the management of foundations, may decide that the risks of incurring penalties under sections 4941(a)(2), 4944 (a)(2) and 4945(a)(2) as foundation managers who "knowingly" participate in proscribed acts are too great.[110]

At a time when foundations will need quality professional staff more than ever, dedicated and industrious people may be frightened away by the risks attending the position of foundation manager, which is defined to include not only officers, directors, trustees and persons having similar positions and responsibilities, but also, with respect to any act or failure to act, employees of the foundation who have authority or responsibility to act on such a matter.[111] If this happens, the quality of foundation management may be impaired, and once again charity and society would be the loser.

---

[108] Simon, "Some Under-Publicized Consequences," pp. 195-197.
[109] "Private Foundations and the 1969 Tax Reform Act," p. 274.
[110] See discussion, pp. 51, 71.
[111] Section 4946(b).

7
CONCLUSION

Although we are in the fifth year of operation under the Tax Reform Act of 1969, few conclusions can yet be drawn as to the act's long-term effects. Final regulations have not been issued under all the foundation provisions, and the auditing process has just begun. Nevertheless, there are some indicators.

First, as a philosophical matter, it is difficult to find fault with a number of the new foundation rules. For example, the absolute proscription on acts of self-dealing and the prohibition of income accumulation may go a long way toward eliminating the view that foundations are simply tax dodges.

Second, there are signs that the executive and legislative branches are aware that portions of the act are in need of further attention. The Ways and Means Committee has reported bills that would have reduced the minimum payout to a more realistic figure (as well as lengthen the transitional period) and permit sales of property to related parties under certain limited circumstances. Also, Treasury officials have offered support for legislation to reduce the rate of the section 4940 tax to a level approximately equal to enforcement costs.

Third, the burden of the act may, in the long run, prove to be more administrative in nature than substantive, at least for the overwhelming majority of foundations that were created solely for charitable purposes.

Fourth, the most serious effect of the act may be its deterrent effect on the creation of new foundations. Though data are still lacking, it is apparent that the birthrate has been slowed to a significant degree.

How accurate these indicators will prove to be must await the test of time. Nevertheless, it is clear that the foundation world, however reasonably the 1969 act is administered, will never be the same.